Environmental Scanning for Strategic Leadership

Patrick M. Callan, *Editor*
Education Commission of the States

NEW DIRECTIONS FOR INSTITUTIONAL RESEARCH

PATRICK T. TERENZINI, *Editor-in-Chief*
University of Georgia

MARVIN W. PETERSON, *Associate Editor*
University of Michigan

Number 52, Winter 1986

Paperback sourcebooks in
The Jossey-Bass Higher Education Series

Jossey-Bass Inc., Publishers
San Francisco • London

Patrick M. Callan (ed.).
Environmental Scanning for Strategic Leadership.
New Directions for Institutional Research, no. 52.
Volume XIII, Number 4.
San Francisco: Jossey-Bass, 1986.

New Directions for Institutional Research
Patrick T. Terenzini, *Editor-in-Chief*
Marvin W. Peterson, *Associate Editor*

New Directions for Institutional Research (publication number USPS 098-830) is published quarterly by Jossey-Bass Inc., Publishers, and is sponsored by the Association for Institutional Research. The volume and issue numbers above are included for the convenience of libraries. Second-class postage paid at San Francisco, California, and at additional mailing offices. POSTMASTER: Send address changes to Jossey-Bass Inc., Publishers, 433 California Street, San Francisco, California 94104.

Editorial correspondence should be sent to the Editor-in-Chief, Patrick T. Terenzini, Institute of Higher Education, University of Georgia, Athens, Georgia 30602.

Library of Congress Catalog Card Number 85-81892

International Standard Serial Number ISSN 0271-0579

International Standard Book Number ISBN 1-55542-987-4

Cover art by WILLI BAUM

Manufactured in the United States of America

Ordering Information

The paperback sourcebooks listed below are published quarterly and can be ordered either by subscription or single-copy.

Subscriptions cost $40.00 per year for institutions, agencies, and libraries. Individuals can subscribe at the special rate of $30.00 per year *if payment is by personal check.* (Note that the full rate of $40.00 applies if payment is by institutional check, even if the subscription is designated for an individual.) Standing orders are accepted.

Single copies are available at $9.95 when payment accompanies order, and *all single-copy orders under $25.00 must include payment.* (California, New Jersey, New York, and Washington, D.C., residents please include appropriate sales tax.) For billed orders, cost per copy is $9.95 plus postage and handling. (Prices subject to change without notice.)

Bulk orders (ten or more copies) of any individual sourcebook are available at the following discounted prices: 10–49 copies, $8.95 each; 50–100 copies, $7.96 each; over 100 copies, *inquire.* Sales tax and postage and handling charges apply as for single copy orders.

Please note that these prices are for the academic year 1986–1987 and are subject to change without prior notice. Also, some titles may be out of print and therefore not available for sale.

To ensure correct and prompt delivery, all orders must give either the *name of an individual* or an *official purchase order number.* Please submit your order as follows:

Subscriptions: specify series and year subscription is to begin.
Single Copies: specify sourcebook code (such as, IR1) and first two words of title.

Mail orders for United States and Possessions, Latin America, Canada, Japan, Australia, and New Zealand to:
Jossey-Bass Inc., Publishers
433 California Street
San Francisco, California 94104

Mail orders for all other parts of the world to:
Jossey-Bass Limited
28 Banner Street
London EC1Y 8QE

New Directions for Institutional Research Series
Patrick T. Terenzini *Editor-in-Chief*
Marvin W. Peterson, *Associate Editor*

IR1 *Evaluating Institutions for Accountability,* Howard R. Bowen
IR2 *Assessing Faculty Effort,* James I. Doi
IR3 *Toward Affirmative Action,* Lucy W. Sells

IR4 *Organizing Nontraditional Study,* Samuel Baskin
IR5 *Evaluating Statewide Boards,* Robert O. Berdahl
IR6 *Assuring Academic Progress Without Growth,* Allan M. Cartter
IR7 *Responding to Changing Human Resource Needs,* Raul Heist, Jonathan R. Warren
IR8 *Measuring and Increasing Academic Productivity,* Robert A. Wallhaus
IR9 *Assessing Computer-Based System Models,* Thomas R. Mason
IR10 *Examining Departmental Management,* James Smart, James Montgomery
IR11 *Allocating Resources Among Departments,* Paul L. Dressel, Lou Anna Kimsey Simon
IR12 *Benefiting from Interinstitutional Research,* Marvin W. Peterson
IR13 *Applying Analytic Methods to Planning and Management,* David S. P. Hopkins, Roger G. Scroeder
IR14 *Protecting Individual Rights to Privacy in Higher Education,* Alton L. Taylor
IR15 *Appraising Information Needs of Decision Makers,* Carl R. Adams
IR16 *Increasing the Public Accountability of Higher Education,* John K. Folger
IR17 *Analyzing and Constructing Cost,* Meredith A. Gonyea
IR18 *Employing Part-Time Faculty,* David W. Leslie
IR19 *Using Goals in Research and Planning,* Robert Fenske
IR20 *Evaluting Faculty Performance and Vitality,* Wayne C. Kirschling
IR21 *Developing a Total Marketing Plan,* John A. Lucas
IR22 *Examining New Trends in Administrative Computing,* E. Michael Staman
IR23 *Professional Development for Institutional Research,* Robert G. Cope
IR24 *Planning Rational Retrenchment,* Alfred L. Cooke
IR25 *The Impact of Student Financial Aid on Institutions,* Joe B. Henry
IR26 *The Autonomy of Public Colleges,* Paul L. Dressel
IR27 *Academic Program Evaluation,* Eugene C. Craven
IR28 *Academic Planning for the 1980s,* Richard B. Heydinger
IR29 *Institutional Assessment for Self-Improvement,* Richard I. Miller
IR30 *Coping with Faculty Reduction,* Stephen R. Hample
IR31 *Evaluation of Management and Planning Systems,* Nick L. Poulton
IR32 *Increasing the Use of Program Evaluation,* Jack Lindquist
IR33 *Effective Planned Change Strategies,* G. Melvin Hipps
IR34 *Qualitative Methods for Institutional Research,* Eileen Kuhns, S. V. Martorana
IR35 *Information Technology: Advances and Applications,* Bernard Sheehan
IR36 *Studying Student Attrition,* Ernest T. Pascarella
IR37 *Using Research for Strategic Planning,* Norman P. Uhl
IR38 *The Politics and Pragmatics of Institutional Research,* James W. Firnberg, William F. Lasher
IR39 *Applying Methods and Techniques of Futures Research,* James L. Morrison, William L. Renfro, Wayne I. Boucher
IR40 *College Faculty: Versatile Human Resources in a Period of Constraint,* Roger G. Baldwin, Robert T. Blackburn
IR41 *Determining the Effectiveness of Campus Services,* Robert A. Scott
IR42 *Issues in Pricing Undergraduate Education,* Larry H. Litten
IR43 *Responding to New Realities in Funding,* Larry L. Leslie
IR44 *Using Microcomputers for Planning and Management Support,* William L. Tetlow
IR45 *Impact and Challenges of a Changing Federal Role,* Virginia Ann Hodgkinson

IR46 *Institutional Research in Transition,* Marvin W. Peterson, Mary Corcoran
IR47 *Assessing Educational Outcomes,* Peter T. Ewell
IR48 *The Use of Data in Discrimination Issues Cases,* William Rosenthal, Bernard Yancey
IR49 *Applying Decision Support Systems in Higher Education,* John Rohrbaugh, Anne Taylor McCartt
IR50 *Measuring Faculty Research Performance,* John W. Creswell
IR51 *Enhancing the Management of Fund Raising,* John A. Dunn, Jr.

The Association for Institutional Research was created in 1966 to benefit, assist, and advance research leading to improved understanding, planning, and operation of institutions of higher education. Publication policy is set by its Publications Board.

For information about the Association for Institutional Research, write:

AIR Executive Office
314 Stone Building
Florida State University
Tallahassee, FL 32306

(904) 644-4470

Contents

Editor's Notes

As society has changed, colleges and universities have adapted, becoming more complex and less insulated from society. The pace of change shows no sign of slowing, and the outlook for postsecondary education is one demanding considerable foresight and adaptability.

Postsecondary planning (statewide and institutional) since World War II has been largely planning for expansion. Expansion has occurred not only because of growth in the adult population but also because of the move from elite to mass higher education—beginning in this country with the G.I. Bill of Rights and extending through the 1960s and the 1970s.

Errors in our estimates have tended to fall on the conservative side of actuality. When enrollments are increasing, the tendency is to underestimate the growth. The resulting surprises, while never welcome, are not such as to require cutbacks, and it has never been considered good form to execute the bearer of better-than-expected news. In contrast, when enrollments shrink, the consequences of failing to anticipate change or of underestimating its magnitude are more immediate, more lasting, and more negative—both for the institution and for the individuals affected. In short, the environment is less forgiving.

In recent years, the paths of institutions have been marked by discontinuities and reversals (many of which are attributable to specific changes in public policy). There is every reason to expect similar changes of direction in the future. Thus, institutional planning will be less a matter of projection or extrapolation of the past than of contingency planning and alternative forecasts.

For the last fifteen years of the forty-year period of growth since World War II, the experts have talked of stability and warned of decline. Meanwhile, the bulk of institutional enrollments has marched onward and upward to this swelling chorus of wolf-criers, perhaps as a testament to higher education's resourcefulness in expanding its appeal to new clienteles. Today, however, the wolf really is at the door for many of us.

The years between 1985 and 1995 will see a decline in the college-age population in all regions of the country, at a time when, presumably, the market is saturated with new offerings. Beyond this trend, for many of us changes in the socioeconomic characteristics of the college-age cohort suggest reduced participation rates as well. By the time the echo of the baby boom reaches us in the 1990s, we will have had to make some difficult choices and to take some unpopular actions.

Perhaps the ultimate test of our planning and management in the face of this enrollment relaxation will be how well our institutions are able to respond to the enrollment growth that will follow in the latter half of the 1990s. In general, we must plan for near-term contraction followed by long-term expansion, but specific institutions will be affected by a welter of environmental influences that have little to do with the general trend. It may be very difficult to discern the mode for institutions, and the norm over this period may apply to hardly any of us. It promises to be an interesting time for institutional researchers and planners.

The bad news for institutional researchers is that their jobs will be more complex. The smaller the service areas of institutions, the more difficult it is to make reliable estimates or projections of their demographic and economic outlooks. The new roles that institutions have added recently to sustain their growth will complicate the job of projecting demand. We shall have to look farther outside individual institutions to detect relevant changes in the environment, and we shall have to look farther into the future to anticipate shifts in our planning assumptions.

The good news for institutional researchers is that their jobs will become more important and that the tools at their disposal will have improved and increased. In the complex environment ahead, extrapolations of recent institutional experience will not be so instructive as in the past. Boards will be forced to look beyond the "bottom line" of total enrollments and to come to some appreciation of the diverse environmental factors that, in composite, form the enrollment outlook. The keepers of this information will become much more visible as important contributors to institutional policy debates. As the price of this visibility, institutional researchers will have to develop facility with a variety of new tools for planning, to complement those already in use. Moreover, educational researchers in general will have to expand their networks of colleagues to encompass demographers and economists outside the educational establishment. We can expect to find that the most instructive lessons for our "industry" are to be learned not from other educational institutions but from other segments of society.

The most urgent task of institutional researchers in this period is to provide the basis for better-informed and more effective leadership of their institutions. This volume is concerned with institutional research in this broad context, as distinguished from the context of institutional marketing. It sees the institution as a leading member of society and as shaping and determining changes, rather than simply reacting to and surviving change.

We begin this volume with an overview of the changing environment of colleges and universities, as seen by Richard W. Jonsen of the Western Interstate Commission for Higher Education (WICHE). Jonsen presents evidence of changes in six primary facets of the environment—demographic, economic, political, organizational, technological, and social-cultural—and raises important questions about them that deserve the attention of institutional researchers and decision makers.

Second, Norman S. Kaufman of WICHE uses data on past enrollment changes as an introduction to projections of the likely number and character of postsecondary clientele in coming years. He also offers advice to institutional research specialists about using such projections.

Third, three economists of education—Larry Leslie of the University of Arizona, Russell Rumberger of Stanford, and William H. Pickens of the California Postsecondary Education Commission (CPEC)—discuss the implications for colleges and universities of current changes in the American economy and in regional, state, and local economies.

Fourth, William H. Pickens offers advice about how to measure changes in institutional finance over time, taking into account the impact of inflation, as measured by different cost indices; changes in workload; and the choice of an appropriate base year for calculating the changes.

Fifth, Robert G. Cope of the University of Washington proposes a "strategic triangle" concept for systematically gathering future-oriented information, first to make wise strategic choices and then to make decisions on institutional guidance and control.

Sixth, Keith G. Pailthorp of CPEC describes strategic planning in three higher education contexts: systemwide (the San Francisco Community College District), institutional (the University of Nevada at Reno), and at the state-agency level (CPEC itself).

Finally, Martin M. Ahumada and JB Lon Hefferlin of CPEC review sources of additional assistance on the topic.

All of us hope that this volume will contribute to more effective institutional research and decision making throughout higher education.

Patrick M. Callan
Editor

Patrick M. Callan is vice-president of the Education Commission of the States. Until mid-1986 he was director of the California Postsecondary Education Commission, California's coordinating council for education beyond high school.

Changes in six major facets of the environment need the attention of institutional research specialists and institutional policy makers.

The Environmental Context for Postsecondary Education

Richard W. Jonsen

According to the *American Heritage Dictionary* (1982), *environment* means "the total of circumstances surrounding an organism or group of organisms, especially (a) combination of external or extrinsic physical conditions that affect and influence the growth and development of organisms; (b) the complex of social and cultural conditions affecting the nature of an individual or community."

Isn't the importance and significance of the environment—this total of circumstances and influences affecting institutions of higher education—self-evident? I believe it is not. Colleges once were fairly insulated institutions, and the period of collegiate education was sharply set off from the secondary education that preceded it and the work life that followed it. This is no longer true. Neither institutions of higher education nor the experiences of their students are as sharply marked off from "the outside world" as they used to be. Today, many students see themselves as workers or family breadwinners to as great an extent as they see themselves as students. Today, many institutions are as concerned with their relationships with the community in its social, political, economic, and cultural

---

I am indebted to four colleagues at WICHE for their thoughtful review of this chapter: Frank Abbott, Erica Gosman, Charles Lenth, and Phillip Sirotkin.

P. M. Callan (ed.). *Environmental Scanning for Strategic Leadership.*
New Directions for Institutional Research, no. 52. San Francisco: Jossey-Bass, Winter 1986.

aspects as they are about their relationships with the community of scholars and students that constitutes their core of participants.

Of equal importance, the environment, the circumstances and conditions external to colleges and universities, now plays a much more active role in the institutions' life and affairs. The student aid policies of federal and state governments and the changing job market their graduating students face are two examples that come quickly to mind.

Keller (1983, p. 145) acknowledges this when he describes the "outward looking" character of strategic planning. He calls such planning the "single most important contribution to organizational decision making," because "three-quarters of all change at most institutions of higher learning is now triggered by outside factors."

Elements in the Environment of Higher Education

Institutions of higher education, and indeed all institutions, perennially swim in this environmental sea of external circumstances. There are six primary aspects of this environment: the demographic environment, the economic environment, the political environment, the organizational environment, the technological environment, and the social and cultural environment.

The institutional system is constantly adapting itself to *demographic* expansion and contraction. The growth of American higher education after World War II was largely a function of the sheer need to accommodate increasing numbers of persons in the college-going age group. The continued existence of so many institutions is a reflection of the assumption of increased financial returns from college attendance (part of the *economic* environment) and the understandable response on the part of high school graduates to that assumption. Public and private institutions have always been embedded in the *political* environment. Political activity dominates the day-to-day activities of the leaders of public institutions, and politically imposed requirements, such as affirmative action, demand the attention of leaders of both public and private institutions. Higher education in the United States is an intensely competitive activity. In the quest for status and resources (important institutional motivators), institutions gauge their success in relation to the other institutions that constitute the *organizational* environment. The *technological* environment is increasingly important: Institutions attempt to understand the manpower demands of "the information society," as they relate to student interests and programmatic requirements, and also to understand the technology itself as it changes modes of instruction, approaches to research, and institutions' link with other institutions and their communities. Finally, the changes in *social* and cultural patterns of students and other participants in collegiate communities have enormous bearings on the resource requirements (for student personnel, staff for residence facilities, and so forth).

To be sure, these environmental elements have always pressed in on colleges and universities, requiring their leaders to be alert and responsive. Is today's context for higher education any different? It is, and I believe that the pace of environmental change is so rapid as to constitute a qualitative difference in the need for institutions to understand these environmental factors and to prepare to adapt to their challenges and opportunities, and that institutions must be structured to do just that. This is not self-evident. As Cameron (1983) has shown, declining institutions appear to reveal an excessive concern for *internal* (administrative) efficiency, rather than for understanding and coping with the environment. Nor is adaptation to the environment automatic. The strategic plans an institution makes are based as much on its history and on the shared beliefs of its participants as on simple or even not-so-simple reactions to environmental change. Thus, institutions do not automatically understand the environment, nor does the environment dictate courses of institutional action. Although we recognize today that the freedom of institutions is in many ways limited by environmental factors, both formally (through governmental regulations) and informally (through fluctuations in demography and economy), institutional latitude to act is not thereby entirely eliminated or even significantly diminished.

Nevertheless, an effective college president cannot fail to recognize that as he or she seeks to compete for both status and resources, the environment sets many of the conditions of that competition, as well as providing the opportunities for action. What are the elements of that environment, and how can an institution best understand them?

The Demographic Environment

Institutional leaders in higher education, over the past decade or so, have been both mesmerized by demographic realities and, ironically, partially blinded to those realities. While recognizing the decline in the numbers of college-age persons, many college and university presidents have nevertheless predicted their institutions' imperviousness to demographic reality. The general pattern of decline, partial recovery, further decline, and recovery in the numbers of students graduating from high school in the United States is quite well known. The geographical variations in that pattern are less well recognized. According to the Western Interstate Commission for Higher Education (WICHE) projections of changes in the number of public high school graduates since 1981 (McConnell and Kaufman, 1984), the nation is likely to experience a 22 percent decline by 1992, but the Northeast may suffer a 35 percent drop and the north central region may see a 29 percent decline, while the southeastern and south central regions and the western region slip by only 11 percent. By 1999, the number of public high school graduates is projected to be 9 percent less than in 1981 for the nation at large, but 30 percent less in the Northeast and 22 percent less in the north central region, 3 percent more than in 1981 in the southeastern and south central regions, and 19 percent more than 1981 in the West.

Moreover, many people think that growth in the adult population, which accompanies a decline in the traditional college-age population, will mean increased enrollments in adult and continuing education that will offset smaller numbers of entering freshmen. But again, less well recognized or appreciated is the fact that this environmental factor must be understood on a very local geographical basis. Adults are much more place-bound than traditional college-age students are, and therefore a college's potential clientele among adults resides primarily in its local "catchment" or service area.

Another overlooked aspect of the demographic environment is the shifting ethnic and socioeconomic composition of the college-going population. Minority students (except Asian Americans) are currently heavily underrepresented in higher education, and that underrepresentation increases at each level in the institutional hierarchy. Yet, in many areas of the country, even as the college-age population decreases, the minority percentage of that population will increase. For example, in California, Hispanic students constituted 22 percent of the population aged twenty to twenty-four in 1980, but in the year 2000 they are expected to represent 33 percent of that same age group (Dolman and Kaufman, 1985). Thus, institutions will miss the mark if they base their enrollment forecasts on national projections of high school graduation rates or on more localized projections undifferentiated by race.

Scanning the demographic environment therefore involves answers to these and other questions:

- What are the short-run demographic trends in the college's catchment or service area?
- What are the characteristics of the college-going age group in that area with respect to high school graduation rates, college graduation rates, types of colleges attended, and so forth?
- What is the ethnic and racial composition of that population, and what are the historical differences among these groups relative to educational achievement?
- What is the socioeconomic composition of that population, and what does that predict about college interests and aptitude of future college-age cohorts?
- What is the size and what are the characteristics of the adult population in the college's immediate geographical service area with respect to educational achievement and socioeconomic status (factors that strongly influence educational participation)?

- If the college's current enrollment is heterogeneous, what are the predominant student prototypes (part-time/full-time, working/nonworking), and how do those fit with the prototypes in the population from which the institution draws?

The Economic Environment

The economy does not exert a direct influence on institutions of higher education. Institutional expenditures are affected by inflation, but apparently at a different rate from widely recognized indicators of inflation, such as the consumer price index. Among those expenditures, the dominant share is for salaries, but aggregate salaries are affected very differently from those of individual groups. For example, it is well known that faculty salaries in "high tech" areas have been driven up by market forces more rapidly than salaries in other disciplines.

Similarly, institutional revenues are affected by a varied set of economic forces. The overall economy even acts on different revenue components in different ways. The recent recession may have caused more students to enroll in community colleges, but that enrollment growth appears to have subsided when the economy improved by the fall of 1984 (Meyer, 1984). At the same time, enrollments at high-cost institutions, at least in the aggregate, do not appear to have been adversely affected by the loss of consumer income among family groups that would be expected to be able to pay high-cost tuitions. State governments, the primary funders of higher education, were affected differently by the recent economic recession. They have recovered from that recession at different rates and, in the ways they fund higher education, have chosen to react to the recession and recovery quite differently. Revenues in some states have still not fully enjoyed the effects of economic recovery felt by the federal government and some states. Aside from state economic conditions, appropriations for higher education over the last decade or so have come into direct competition with those for other state services. As a result, the portion of state appropriations dedicated to higher education has declined.

Other major sources of institutional revenue are also affected by economic conditions. Students' ability to pay tuition at whatever level is affected by the economy, as are philanthropic contributions. The latter are, of course, significantly affected by federal tax policies.

An even more complex aspect of the economic environment of higher education is the structure of that economy with respect to employment and jobs. As we know, each state and region presents a different profile in terms of the ways in which various industries (manufacturing, service, information industries, "high tech" manufacturing firms) are represented in its economy. In the last few years, states relying heavily in their work forces on natural resources and extractive industries or on such traditional heavy manufacturers as the steel industry have sought aggressively to diversify their economic bases (for example, through the recruitment of high-technology firms). The changing structure of the job market in a college's service area has enormous implications for the kinds of potential students a college, especially a public one, will find in its immediate pool, including the kinds of people who may be seeking continuing professional education. Considerable sophistication is required to keep up with these changes and to predict changes likely to take place.

Offsetting the complexity of economic influences on higher education is the ability of most institutions, at least those of medium size or larger, to understand and even to forecast fluctuations in the economic environment with some sophistication. Chief finance officers, budget officers, development officers, and economists on the faculty should all contribute to the institution's capacity to understand its economic environment and adapt its policies accordingly.

In understanding its economic environment, a college or university must ask such questions as:

- What is the general economic condition of our service area and its region?
- What are the short- and long-term economic trends in our area?
- What is the current manpower situation in our service area, and how is it likely to change with respect both to employment rates and to the structure of the job market?
- What are the trends in personal income?
- What are the trends in revenues of local, state, and federal governments as they affect our funding, and what are the claims on those revenue sources from other government-funded functionaries?
- What are the trends in state and federal tax policies as they affect philanthropic contributions?
- What are the possibilities for economic growth and for change in the structure of employment—locally, regionally, and nationally—as they may affect enrollment and financial support?
- What are the implications for private colleges and universities of the increased fundraising efforts on the part of public institutions?

The Political Environment

It is recognized by those who work in higher education, if not by the general public, that colleges and universities are intimately involved in the political environment. Public institutions, especially smaller ones and nonresearch institutions, derive most of their funding from state government and thus are deeply involved in the budget process in their states. While the state portion is less for major public research universities, the magnitude of dollars to fund those institutions means that they represent a substantial proportion of a state's outlay. Although private institutions are less dependent on state funds, state support for them, especially through student financial aid, has increased over the past two decades. Thus, of necessity, both public and private institutions, acting either individually or in concert through their state boards or associations, are thoroughly involved in the political processes in their states.

At the federal level, the influence of political decisions is important to higher education, but in different ways for different kinds of institutions. All institutions are affected by federal financial aid policies. Especially since the late 1960s, federal education policy has been largely (although not exclusively) focused on the various student aid programs. Research policies are of interest to a smaller group of institutions, and critically so to a hundred or so major research universities. Increasingly, institutions are represented politically through their Washington-based associations, and because each of those associations represents a clientele with a very different set of institutional interests, it has been extremely difficult for the higher education community in Washington to achieve consensus on federal higher education policy.

Public institutions also participate in the political process through appointments to their governing boards. As colleges and universities have become more important social institutions, those appointments have tended to become somewhat more political. At the same time, the governance of institutions has been influenced by open-meeting laws, freedom of information acts, interest-group representation, and other moves toward consumerism and greater citizen empowerment.

Thus, the political environment poses a number of questions that institutions cannot ignore such as:

- What are the political dynamics of the state, and how are those dynamics represented at the local level (that is, by the representatives in the college's district)?
- What are the national political dynamics, and how are they represented locally?
- How does the institution involve itself politically at the state and national level: directly (this may be the case at the state level) or through state or national associations?
- What is the mechanism for the state's decision making in higher education, and what branches other than the legislative and the executive are involved (state fiscal agencies, state higher education coordinating agencies, and so forth)?

The Organizational Environment

Every college and university exists in an environment that, depending on the college's geographical area and influence, includes neighboring and perhaps distant institutions, both public and private. This environment has to be understood in its potential both for competition (especially the price competition of public institutions and the status competition of private institutions) and for cooperation (especially among other private institutions and coordinated planning endeavors).

Higher education has become increasingly "permeable," in the sense of the increased ability and inclination of students to move back and forth among institutions: between collegiate institutions and educational activities in the noncollegiate sector (corporate training programs, for example) and between education and work or different combinations of both. This is both a cultural and an educational phenomenon. The rise in the number of part-time students in American colleges and universities dramatizes the fact that college-going is no longer a full-time occupation to be pursued only until one receives a degree. The increasing numbers of adults in higher education also dramatizes the fact that the college experience is no longer reserved for eighteen- to twenty-two-year-olds. However, this permeability is also an educational phenomenon in that the educational system increasingly needs to be structured so that certain parts articulate with others, as for some time the two-year institutions have articulated (however imperfectly) with four-year institutions to accommodate the transfer of students seeking baccalaureate degrees.

The powerful drive for status has made the individualism and competitiveness of institutions a primary feature of higher education. As the institutional system grows more complex, more permeable, and more interdependent, institutions will need to recognize the importance of substituting for that competition (or at least accompanying it with) cooperation and linkages with other institutions of higher education, other educational providers in the noncollegiate sector, and other business and political organizations. The insularity of American colleges and universities has probably never been a very good thing for students; it may also be increasingly bad for the institutions themselves.

With regard to economic institutions, there is much current discussion of the fact that the employers of higher education's "products" are, of course, part of higher education's organizational environment, in the sense both of manpower requirements and of their links with the delivery system. Thus, the organizational environment of an institution of higher education prompts such questions as:

- What are the relevant other higher education institutions in the college's or university's service area (local, statewide, regional, or national)?
- What is the quality of the institution's relationships with these other institutions? Do they tend to be competitive or cooperative? Are those relationships conducive to meeting the institution's needs and goals?

- What is the institution's relationship (and needed relationship) with the elementary and secondary school districts?
- What is the institution's relationship with professional associations and accrediting bodies?
- What is the institution's relationship (or needed relationship) with other educational providers, including corporate training programs?
- What is the institution's relationship with the corporations and government agencies that hire its graduates?
- What is the institution's relationship with quasi-political agencies (such as regulatory agencies) that relate to it formally or informally?

The Technological Environment

The speed and magnitude of technological change in our society could bring about proposed changes in the operations of colleges and universities. The development of new instruments (such as interactive videodiscs), new delivery systems (such as cable and low-power television), and new means of distance delivery (such as satellite), as well as the mass production of what once were large-scale and expensive facilities (such as computers), contain profound implications for the ways in which higher education does business. These implications include new attempts to separate instruction from certification, the possibility of significant changes in the economics of higher education (from labor-intensive instruction to capital-intensive instruction), new roles for faculty members and changes in their relationships with students, and a diminished role for the campus as the place where higher education occurs.

These changes may or may not happen. However, there is powerful evidence that institutions are rapidly assimilating new technologies (especially computers) into their instructional programs and developing or planning the development of integrated electronic delivery systems, both on and off campus, the investment in which could affect future budget decisions. Institutions are in fact taking advantage of the enormous potential and flexibility of information technologies.

Practice, though, is far outstripping both planning and policy making, and institutions are hard pressed to understand the future as it relates to the role information technologies will play in the delivery of instruction, as well as in the conduct of research and administration in higher education. Information technologies also present new opportunities—and perhaps a far greater need for cooperation and coordination among institutions—that are not yet fully realized. These opportunities and imperatives are implied in such questions as:

- What is the information society, and does the rapid development of new ways to deliver, represent, and process information foreshadow a general social or cultural revolution?

- What are the educational implications of that revolution?
- Is the institution in the mainstream of the information society?
- Does the institution have formal academic programs that need to adapt themselves to changes in information technologies brought about by the information age?
- What use does the institution make of computers, and what future use is demanded by changes in student interests and needed access to training?
- What improvements in the efficiency or effectiveness of instructional operation can be gained by joining with other institutional providers through the capabilities of the new information technologies?
- How will the information revolution alter the structure and function of the library?
- What new markets can be opened up through the institution's employment of new technology to reach off-campus students?

The Social Environment

Colleges have been used to dealing in a social environment that was fairly homogeneous, drawing students from a single socioeconomic stratum, a single religious background, or a single geographical region. The democratization of access (especially through federal financial aid), the diversification of programs, and the fierce competition for students in recent years have made the social environment reasonably complex. It is more essential, although difficult, for every college today to understand the social environment in its present dimensions and, even more important, to try to understand likely changes in that environment (for example, in student tastes with respect to programs of study and college climates) in order to cope with those changes more effectively.

Preparing an institution to cope with the future is difficult. It is even more difficult if one adopts the view of the future held by such observers as Toffler (1980), who argues that "humanity faces a quantum leap forward . . . the deepest social upheaval and creative restructuring of all times. Without clearly recognizing it, we are engaged in building a remarkable new civilization from the ground up." Profound changes in social organization, attitudes, and life-styles are also documented by Naisbitt (1982), Yankelovich (1982), and Ferguson (1980). Recently, researchers at the Stanford Research Institute have attempted to define nine American life-styles that relate to very different values, motivations, and experiences and that could describe different patterns of education and educational interest (Mitchell, 1983).

The soft data represented by some of these information sources can imply hard choices relative to resource allocation. The increasing vocationalism of students translates today into enormous shifts of faculty and faculty loads from humanities and social sciences to business and engineering. Trends toward a more flexible mix of work-leisure education contain similar implications for higher education.

The implications for institutions of much of this theorizing and categorizing are difficult to sort out. Soft social science analysis fits poorly into hard decision making. Yet, the fuzziness of futurizing and of journalistic analyses of social trends should not cause us to dismiss them as unimportant. The vocationalism of today's college students, which was identified in trend analyses by astute observers of higher education in the late 1970s, has led to difficult resource allocation decisions. Thus, an institution's social environment raises such questions as:

- What are the trends and countertrends in the social milieu?
- What are the larger cultural trends that will influence the nature of higher education?
- What is the changing socioeconomic composition of the population in the institution's geographical environment, and what are the implications of this, for the institution, in terms of student preferences related to academic programs and campus social climate?

The Turbulent Environments of Colleges and Universities

The distinguishing characteristic of higher education's current environment is turbulence. Never before has higher education had to cope with such a diverse array of factors. Changing birth rates of the past several decades have left us a legacy of sharp fluctuations in the size of the college-age group, just at a time when adults, particularly women, have returned to the campus in unprecedented numbers. Simultaneously, society is experiencing differing birth rates among certain segments of the population, a development that has profound implications for enrollment and service demands.

The spectacular growth of information technologies in our economy over the past ten years, and the likely increase in the rate of that growth in the future, pose enormous challenges to higher education. These challenges will test institutions' ability to produce specialized manpower for the industrial sector and their ability to adjust their curricula to provide the necessary training for all students in certain of these technologies (for example, computer literacy), as well as to make the most efficient and effective use of new information technologies.

For many institutions, the organizational environment has changed rapidly in the last few years, as institutions whose principal business is not education have developed training programs and as colleges have attempted to cope more successfully with their relationships with other institutions in both the educational and corporate sectors.

Equally rapid and turbulent changes could be described in the other aspects of the environment. The point here is simply to demonstrate the obvious: College and universities are challenged as never before in their understanding of and need to adapt to these changes. Yet neither the internal structure of institutions, the mechanisms linking them to the environment, nor the processes of deliberation for decision making have themselves changed sufficiently to facilitate such understanding and adaptation.

Structures for Scanning the Environment

Some necessary elements for defining and understanding the environment are already in place. As has been pointed out, colleges and universities have administrative officers, such as chief financial officers, budget officers, and development officers, whose responsibilities include developing a thorough understanding of the economic environment in which their institutions operate and of the effects that changes in this environment are likely to have on revenues and expenditures. Admissions officers typically possess a reasonably sophisticated understanding of changes in demographics, as those changes are likely to affect their institutions. Especially when operating decisions are involved, an institution can be expected to have a good understanding of environmental factors. Interest rates affecting short-term investments, high school graduation rates in the institution's state or "catchment area" (as they affect next year's freshman class), changes in tax laws (as they affect the philanthropic decisions of the major donors)—a well-run institution should have access to such information on a day-to-day basis.

However, having access to a piece of the environmental picture, especially in the short run, does not mean that an institution necessarily has access to information about larger factors that will influence the long-run operation of the institution. Having information about the economic and demographic environment does not automatically imply having access to information about the other environmental aspects we have discussed. Finally, even if an institution has access to information about all aspects of the environment we have described, it does not necessarily follow that it has an adequate mechanism for an integrated understanding of the environment as a whole. What is needed, then, is:

- A mechanism to integrate understanding about various aspects of the environment, especially as they might be interrelated
- The capacity to translate this integrated understanding into the institution's long-range planning and decision making
- Sufficiently high-level priority given to this activity to ensure its translation into decisions and then implementation.

As we approach what is likely to be the "trough" of the demographic environment (the low point of high school graduation rates in the

United States will be reached in 1991), with complications from a period of rapid technological and other change, institutions need to be structurally prepared for the job of environmental scanning, so that necessary adaptations can be identified and implemented. Responsibility for such environmental scanning can be lodged in a number of different places, but provision should be made for sufficiently short-circuit access to the president and the governing board. This responsibility could be placed in:

- The office of institutional research, which routinely collects much of this data for operating reports, but which would in many cases need to be broadened in its scope of responsibility to become an office with genuine capacity for environmental scanning.
- An executive assistant to the president, who could have responsibility for pulling together the information trends and possibilities from various offices.
- A faculty committee composed of people whose areas of expertise (economics, political science, sociology, computer science) bear on these environments. Such a committee would offer a fairly high level of sophistication but would need the authority or influence to place environmental scanning in a decision framework.
- An office already responsible for scanning part of the environment (for example, the admissions office, in its responsibility for understanding the demographic environment), an office that could be given the added responsibility (along with some resources) to integrate that understanding with other aspects of the environment.

Whatever the structure, it is important that environmental scanning receive consistent attention from the highest level of institutional policy makers, both administrators (the president and other key officers) and the governing board. An important part of the regular effort at board development should include sessions devoted to understanding both environmental change and those institutional changes necessary to maintain or successfully change the institution's niche in that environment.

We underestimate the extent to which sophisticated and shrewd understanding of the environment has been a key component of institutional leadership in the United States. Effective college and university presidents have always known the environmental sea in which they were swimming: other organizations, their key political constituencies, the changing numbers and nature of student clientele, alumni, and other groups. What has changed today is the scope and complexity of the environment, a scope and complexity that can no longer be embraced by a single well-informed individual. There now need to be a structure and a process dedicated to gaining that understanding and relating it effectively to the decision-making processes of the institution.

Conclusion

A warning is in order. To say that the institution must have the capacity both to understand the changing environment in a sophisticated way and to integrate that understanding effectively into its decision-making process is not at all to say that an understanding of the environment and the suggested constraints or opportunities that it might present should dictate the institution's course of action. As the environment becomes a stronger factor in institutional decision making, so too must we foster a sophisticated and sensitive understanding of the institution's history and the bedrock principles on which it operates educationally. It is not evident that institutions are likely to do this. Many smaller institutions have responded to environmental change, or at least to what they thought was environmental change, by flailing about to find new markets, new roles, new opportunities for income, and new links with other kinds of organizations. Some of this activity has been imaginative, but much of it has been educationally questionable. At the same time, some institutions, have acted as though an organization, or an individual for that matter, can ignore historical commitments and philosophical beliefs with impunity.

One of the great lessons to be learned from the growth and development of American higher education in the last forty years is that there is a price for growth and even for well-motivated response to new challenges. Increased access has had its price; so have responsiveness to social problems, the development of closer ties with industry and greater attention to economic development, and the press for research productivity in the quest for institutional status. That quest for status, for example, has sometimes loosened the institutional "gyroscopes" that are simultaneously one of American higher education's most frustrating aspects (its iron-fisted adherence to tradition) and one of its great strengths.

American higher education has responded to the challenges imposed by the environment of these last two or three decades flexibly and energetically, often admirably. Still, changes in the environment, as the United States approaches the year 2000, will test as never before our institutional character and commitments as we try both understand and to cope with change.

References

The American Heritage Dictionary. (2nd ed.) Boston: Houghton Mifflin, 1982.

Cameron, K. "Strategic Responses to Conditions of Decline." *Journal of Higher Education,* 1983, *54,* 359–380.

Dolman, G., Jr., and Kaufman, N. S. *Minorities in Higher Education: The Changing Southwest (California).* Boulder, Colo.: Western Interstate Commission for Higher Education, 1985.

Ferguson, M. *The Aquarian Conspiracy: Personal and Social Transformation in the 1980s.* Los Angeles: Tarcher, 1980.

Keller, G. *Academic Strategy.* Baltimore: Johns Hopkins University Press, 1983.
McConnell, W. R., and Kaufman, N. S. *High School Graduates: Projections for the Fifty States (1982–2000).* Boulder, Colo.: Western Interstate Commission for Higher Education, 1984.
Meyer, J. "2-Year Colleges Facing Serious Enrollment Decline." *The Chronicle of Higher Education,* November 7, 1984, p. 3.
Mitchell, A. *The Nine American Lifestyles.* New York: Warner, 1983.
Naisbitt, J. *Megatrends: Ten New Directions Tranforming Our Lives.* New York: Warner, 1982.
Toffler, A. *The Third Wave.* New York: Bantam, 1980.
Yankelovich, D. *New Rules: Searching for Self-Fulfillment in a World Turned Upside Down.* New York: Bantam, 1982.

Richard W. Jonsen is deputy director of the Western Interstate Commission for Higher Education.

Changes in the age, geographical, racial, and ethnic composition of the United States' population will make it increasingly difficult to project postsecondary enrollments.

Shifts in Postsecondary Clientele

Norman S. Kaufman

As higher education contends with the long-awaited and ill-prepared-for downturn in the numbers of college-age youth, it is becoming increasingly clear that individual institutions of higher education will experience changes in their potential student clientele that vary widely from those suggested by the conventional wisdom.

The aging of the baby-boom cohort, interstate migration from the northeastern and midwestern regions to the Sunbelt, declining fertility rates and family size for middle- and upper-income whites, and increasing fertility rates and family size for selected other population groups are just some of the demographic forces that affect the potential number of students for institutions of postsecondary education.

Clearly, as demographic trends vary by location—within states, between states, and between regions—their effects on the pool of prospective students at particular institutions will also vary greatly. In order to support sound institutional planning and policy development, institutional researchers and planners will need to gain a comprehensive understanding of the demographic environments of their institutions and how they differ from the environments of other institutions in the state, region, and nation.

Many would agree that the expansion of higher education in the period from 1950 to 1980, which resulted in a diverse constellation of institutions serving a broad range of students, occurred largely in response to demographic changes and to resulting societal demands for broadening of access, to include "new" students and to accommodate greater rates of participation by "traditional" students. Current and prospective demographic trends pertaining to postsecondary education are easier to discern if we view these changes against the backdrop of higher education enrollment trends in the post-World War II United States, focusing briefly on several dimensions of expanded student access and institutional growth.

Postsecondary Expansion

While World War II veterans constituted the first contingent of new students in American higher education, increased access to postsecondary education for women has had significant and long-lasting effects on postsecondary enrollments. As recently as the fall of 1963, women comprised 38 percent of total enrollment nationwide. By the fall of 1982, women comprised 51 percent of total enrollment and nearly one-half of graduate enrollment in the United States (Grant and Snyder, 1984, p. 93). Most of the recent incremental growth in postsecondary enrollments can be attributed to increases in the number of women. In the future, postsecondary planners may expect men and women to exhibit similar behaviors with respect to enrollment in colleges, universities, and other postsecondary institutions, as decades of playing "catch up" have culminated in overall parity among the sexes. Planners should note, however, that women students in higher education are still underrepresented in many states and localities and among students from racial and ethnic minority groups. Thus, while some institutions may continue to see proportionately more women among their prospective students, others will notice that the proportion of women approximates that of men.

Postsecondary education has also seen increased numbers of minorities, adults, and nondegree students. Whether these trends continue will be a function of educational policy, finance, and population demographics. In the past, however, institutions have tended to expand to meet the market demands placed on them by these new groups of students. The expansion of the postsecondary education system in the United States after World War II accommodated not only returning veterans but also successive waves of baby boomers, women, minorities, and older students. Institutions in all sectors have expanded to meet this unprecedented push for access to postsecondary education.

Institutional Responses

Over the last twenty-five years, colleges, universities, and proprietary schools have increased in number and grown in size to accommodate enrollment demand. This growth occurred across all segments of postsecondary education. Between 1965 and 1966, and 1982 and 1983, for example, the number of publicly controlled institutions increased by 525, 444 of them two-year colleges. Privately controlled institutions increased in number, too, with 366 new colleges and universities opening their doors between 1965 and 1966, and 1982 and 1983 (Grant and Snyder, 1984, p. 110). Actual college closures have been surprisingly few to date, which suggests that colleges and universities have been surprisingly resilient in responding to students' enrollment preferences and ability to pay.

The remainder of this chapter accepts this last point as axiomatic and proceeds from it; that is, institutions of postsecondary education will attempt to adapt to their changing environments, and as educational and social institutions, they both respond to and cultivate client demands. Academic leaders and planners at all postsecondary institutions need to understand such basic demographic patterns as these among their clientele and formulate academic programs and other initiatives in light of these patterns and their institution's own unique educational missions.

Changing Institutional Environments

To speak of basic demographic patterns is not to suggest that the demographic environments of all states, regions, localities, or institutions will be uniform. Nevertheless, it is useful to understand several general demographic patterns across the nation in order to highlight the significant variations that educational planners must consider.

The first major change is the general aging of the population as the postwar baby-boom generation moves into middle age. In 1982, for example, the median age of the population was at an all-time high of 30.6 years and climbing. Between 1964, which is considered to be the end of the baby boom, and 1979, birth rates fell considerably. The effects of this decline in birth rates are being seen currently in declining school enrollments, diminishing numbers of high school graduates, and small cohorts of traditional college-age youth. However, as Harold Hodgkinson (1983, p. 1) cautions, planners and analysts need to consider both regional differences and racial and ethnic variations of this more pervasive trend. Institutional planners, who are most aware of their particular environments, are in the best position to assess the effects of population changes on their institutions' academic programs and fiscal health.

Individual institutions will be affected not only by the general aging of the population but also by regional variations in the size of the traditional college-age population and its racial and ethnic mix, by the educational and economic aspirations of their clientele, and by public policy regarding access to postsecondary education, especially student financial aid and tuition. Because traditional college-age youth still constitutes the primary clientele of most colleges and universities, an examination of long-term demographic shifts in postsecondary clientele should begin with the eighteen- to twenty-four-year-old cohort.

Traditional College-Age Youth

The population aged eighteen- to twenty-four years is now at an all-time high of approximately 30.4 million (Spencer, 1984, pp. 6–7), which, incidentally, probably explains why we have not yet witnessed widespread declines in college enrollment. Census Bureau projections for this age group (Spencer, 1984, p. 7) show a decline of more than seven million (or almost one-quarter) during the next fifteen years because of the aging of the last cohorts of the baby-boom generation. Middle-series census projections show a rebound in this age group, to 24.6 million people in the year 2000 and to 27.7 million people in 2010. Thereafter, middle-series projections have the eighteen- to twenty-four-year-old group fluctuating between 24 and 28 million persons, never again reaching the 1982 level of 30 million. Under even the highest projection series, which includes unrealistically high assumptions of fertility and immigration, the number of eighteen- to twenty-four-year-olds would not exceed the current national level until the year 2010. These data make it clear that planners must contend with the effects of the receding baby-boom cohorts for at least the next twenty-five years, before they begin to observe an orderly succession of age cohorts through the population.

Traditional Freshmen

Over the next two decades, the population of eighteen- and nineteen-year-olds will mimic the decrease of the larger eighteen- to twenty-four-year-old group. Since some 90 to 94 percent of full-time college freshmen are aged eighteen to nineteen, postsecondary planners and policy makers cannot ignore these trends. The number of eighteen- and nineteen-year-olds, the leading edge of the larger eighteen- to twenty-four-year-old cohort, peaked in 1980, at a level of 8.8 million, and is expected to decline rapidly to 7.4 million in 1985 and to 6.6 million in 1995. By the year 2000, the number of eighteen- and nineteen-year-olds will return to a level of about 7.5 million but will not increase significantly beyond that in succeeding years.

These data suggest a national environment in which the overall declines of traditional college-age youth will be only partially offset in the late 1990s by population growth. However, it is now clear, as we will see in greater detail later, that the racial, ethnic, and geographical composition of the traditional college-age group will depart markedly from the past.

High School Graduates

Nowhere is the significance of these changes in population more apparent to higher education than in the recent history and projections of high school graduates. Discussion of trends and projections of high school graduates also permits a closer examination of differences in state and regional demographic trends like birth rates and migration, as well as of important differences among racial and ethnic groups.

Nationally, the trend line of high school graduates over time parallels (at about 70 percent) the pattern of live births eighteen years earlier. Thus, we can expect the number of high school graduates to decline, from a high of around 3 million in 1978–1979 to a low of around 2.3 million in 1991–1992 (McConnell and Kaufman, 1984, p. 29). By 1998–1999, the number of graduates nationwide will rebound, to a level of 2.6 million. We might expect slight annual increases thereafter, following the trend in the population of eighteen- to twenty-four-year-olds.

The significant point to be drawn from this discussion for postsecondary planning is the dramatic geographical redistribution of high school graduates and, hence, of the traditional college clientele among states and regions of the nation. Although all states and regions face (or already are experiencing) declines in high school graduates, many states in the Southwest and the Far West will see the number of graduates bottom out earlier and will then experience absolute increases over previously established highs. At the same time, other states will experience declines over a longer period and recoveries that never again approach the levels of high school graduates seen in the late 1970s.

Figures 1 and 2 depict the projected number of high school graduates for the United States and for the four regions, respectively. By 1999, the numbers of high school graduates in the western region (Alaska, Arizona, California, Colorado, Hawaii, Idaho, Montana, Nevada, New Mexico, Oregon, Utah, Washington, and Wyoming) and in the southeastern-south central region (Alabama, Arkansas, Florida, Georgia, Kentucky, Louisiana, Mississippi, North Carolina, Oklahoma, South Carolina, Tennessee, Texas, Virginia, and West Virginia) are projected to exceed their actual numbers in 1981, while the northeastern and north central regions fall far below their earlier levels. Yet even these regional projections mask variations among individual states, which warrant more detailed analysis.

By 1994, the states of the northeastern region (Connecticut, Delaware, Maine, Maryland, Massachusetts, New Hampshire, New Jersey, New York, Pennsylvania, Rhode Island, and Vermont) plus the District of Columbia can expect to see high school graduating classes that are 35 percent lower than that of 1981. In 1999, the high school graduating class in this region will remain 30 percent smaller than the class of 1981. The states in the northeastern region can expect to see some variations among

Figure 1. United States Projections, Total High School Grads, 1983–1999

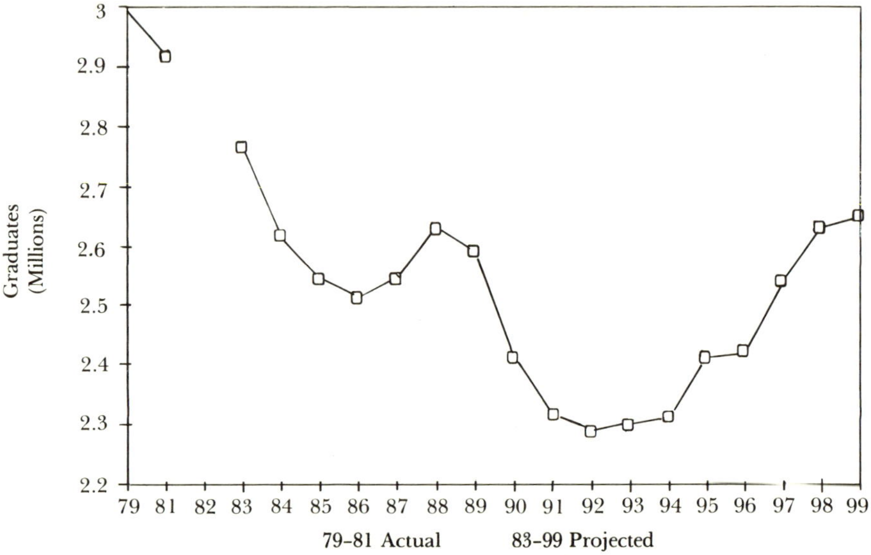

Figure 2. Regional Projections, High School Graduates, 1983–1999

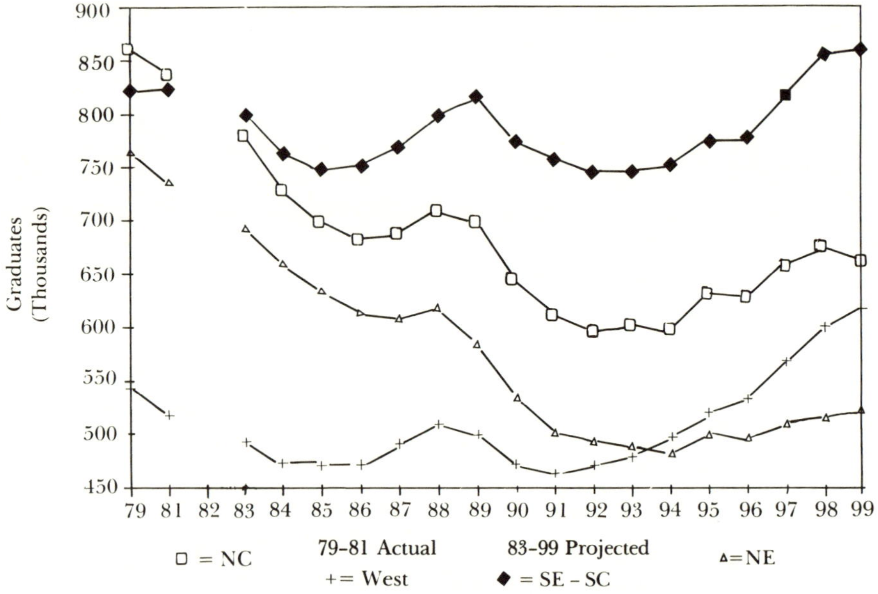

Source: McConnell and Kaufman, 1984, p. 6.

themselves, but the principal trend is one of decline in most of these states, followed by depressed levels of graduates for the foreseeable future (McConnell and Kaufman, 1984, pp. 10–11).

The states of the north central region (Illinois, Indiana, Iowa, Kansas, Michigan, Minnesota, Missouri, Nebraska, North Dakota, Ohio, South Dakota, and Wisconsin) can expect to see a situation similar to that of the northeastern states. Again, while we can expect variations among states, the number of high school graduates in 1999 will remain, on the average, 22 percent below the 1981 level and will probably continue at that level. In part, these data reflect the larger population shift from the Frostbelt to the Sunbelt, but they reflect as well the decline in the number of traditional college-age youth.

One of the key tenets of postsecondary planning in the next twenty years is the need to develop data tailored to the needs and circumstances of individual institutions, rather than relying on broad-brush general profiles. The differences among states within these regions may often be as striking as variations between the regions. While many analysts recognize the potential for explosive postsecondary enrollment growth in the states of Texas and Florida, for example, planners would err to assume that neighboring states necessarily will share in that growth. Since institutions draw students from definable geographical regions, institutional analysts need to use detailed data on each state (or smaller region) from which they draw students. Detailed projections and supporting data on high school graduates by state are available from the Western Interstate Commission on Higher Education (see McConnell and Kaufman, 1984, p. 2).

Race and Ethnicity

Institutional planners and analysts must also take into account widespread changes in the racial and ethnic composition of the population, especially of the younger cohorts. The changing racial and ethnic character of the population overlaps partially with the geographical changes described previously, making it almost impossible to discuss regional differences in the traditional college-age cohorts without also discussing the changes in their racial and ethnic composition. Hodgkinson (1983) argues that higher education analysts have systematically ignored the rapidly increasing percentage of minorities in American public schools and the influence of higher fertility rates among the nonwhite population in contributing to the changing clientele of postsecondary institutions.

These trends may be illustrated by data from the 1980 decennial census. In California, for example, two-thirds of the state's 1980 population was white and non-Hispanic. In contrast, only a little more than half the population under five years of age, and 56 percent of persons aged five to fourteen years, were non-Hispanic whites. By 1995, California's school-age population will consist mostly of nonwhite children. Clearly, postsecondary institutions in California and in other states will find that their prospective students (whether greater or lesser in number) are increasingly nonwhite. In the southwestern states, including California, there will be large proportions of college-age Hispanic students by the year 2000. Other states may witness increased proportions of blacks, Asians, American Indians, and other ethnic groups among their principal postsecondary clienteles.

These patterns will vary by state, region, and locality. Inner-city high schools, for example, may experience lesser enrollment drops than high schools will in more affluent suburbs, because minority groups, with higher rates of fertility, tend to cluster in urban centers. New York City serves as an example of this point. Between 1982 and 1992, the New York State Education Department expects the total number of high school graduates in New York City to decline by only 20 percent, as compared to a statewide decline of over 30 percent. During this period, the percentage of nonwhite high school graduates will increase, forming a majority of the total number of graduates in the city, because of a slower rate of decline in the size of the minority youth population (Regents of the State of New York, 1984, p. 176). Thus, while generalizations are difficult to support in this context, it is safe to say that postsecondary institutions must become increasingly aware of their potential effects on college attendance. Although the overall composition of the population may shift in many states toward a greater concentration of minorities, this may not be reflected totally in the numbers of minority-group high school graduates.

High School Completion

Astin (1982) described what he termed "the educational pipeline for minorities," which he used to compare the educational progress of members of various minority groups. Astin's data revealed that only 55 percent of Chicanos, Puerto Ricans, and American Indians completed high school, as compared to 72 percent of blacks and 83 percent of whites. A recent analysis of data on high school enrollments in Texas and Colorado (Dolman and Kaufman, 1984) revealed that lower percentages of black and Hispanic than white ninth-graders persisted to high school graduation. A similar study in New York (Regents of the State of New York, 1984) showed a similar pattern, comparing twelfth-grade enrollments with ninth-grade enrollments three years earlier. As the racial and ethnic composition of the college-age population changes, institutions may find fewer potential students in the pool of eligible graduates.

These findings suggest that postsecondary institutions face a "double whammy." First, the size of the traditional college-age cohort will shrink while becoming more ethnically diverse. Second, because Hispanics, blacks, and American Indians have shown lower high school completion rates, the effective size of the traditional pool could become even smaller. Clearly, we all have a stake in improving the persistence and preparation of disadvantaged groups. Broad social and educational initiatives will be needed to assist potential dropouts to remain in school and improve their educational standing. In this interest, postsecondary institutions will need to develop closer ties to secondary schools in order to promote better articulation and more meaningful education.

Participation Rates

The enormous growth in postsecondary enrollment throughout the 1960s and the 1970s was driven by the combination of the increasing size of successive college-age cohorts and by dramatic increases in participation rates, first of men and then of women and minorities. Fishlow (1982) summarized the growth in the participation rates of eighteen- to twenty-four-year-olds:

Year	*Participation Rate*	*Year*	*Participation Rate*
1950	10.1%	1975	25.2%
1955	11.2%	1976	25.7%
1960	16.1%	1977	25.2%
1965	22.1%	1978	24.4%
1970	23.9%	1979	24.2%

Several points about these figures are worth noting. First, participation rates for women increased more than for men over this period and have reached the point where men and women enroll at about the same rates. Second, although participation rates for blacks and Hispanics are increasing, they still lag behind the rates for whites. Third, expansion in sectors of the economy that traditionally do not require college education for employment may dampen future participation in postsecondary education or stimulate movement from the traditional collegiate sector to the military or to noncollegiate postsecondary institutions specializing in vocational training.

U.S. Census Bureau estimates (1984, p. 1) show that the number of college students of all ages increased by three million in the decade from 1972 to 1982. Half of the increase resulted from growth in the eligible age pool of applicants. On top of that, the participation rates of women rose so sharply that women accounted for four-fifths of the total enrollment increase. The relatively small increase in enrollment of men in the 1970s, in contrast to the 1960s, appears to be related to the end of the Vietnam war, during which participation rates for males increased drastically.

These data do not tell us, however, what participation rates for men and women will be in the future. Now that women have achieved virtual parity of access, postsecondary planners may reasonably assume that enrollment increases, which were driven by women, will moderate. Unless some other "driver" emerges, the prospects for postsecondary enrollment increases may be quite limited. Without some dramatic change in participation, the demographics will not fuel growth.

If societal pressure for equality of access to postsecondary education for minorities continues, then minority-group members may become the primary "new" clientele in postsecondary education in the years to come. As noted earlier, over the next twenty years—and beyond that—larger percentages of traditional college-age youth will be members of minority groups, especially those who identify themselves as Hispanic. Since the college enrollment rates of blacks and Hispanics lag behind enrollment rates for whites, we may expect to see increases in minority enrollment take hold in much the same manner as increases in women's enrollment have done, with greater rates of participation superimposed on a growing age cohort. In 1982, 27.2 percent of whites between the ages eighteen and twenty-four were enrolled in college, as compared to 19.8 percent of blacks and 16.8 percent of Hispanics (who may be members of any race). If members of these groups can surmount the economic and social barriers to postsecondary education, they will certainly represent a new "driver" of postsecondary enrollments.

Institutional planners should recognize, from a purely demographic perspective, that it is becoming increasingly risky to extrapolate enrollment trends from the status quo and historical trends. Blacks and Hispanics, and other racial and ethnic minorities as well, are distributed unevenly through the United States population. They tend to cluster geographically in several regions of the country and within metropolitan areas, most often in central cities, so that even if their participation rates do increase significantly, not all institutions, regions, or states can expect to see increased enrollments.

Some of the differences between participation rates for whites and minorities, at least among traditional college-age students, can be attributed to differences in family income. Using data from the Current Population Survey, Frances (1982) demonstrates that the college-going rate for students from families whose 1980 incomes were over $25,000 was three times the rate for students from families with incomes under $10,000. These disparities existed in 1980 despite significant gains in participation made by students in the lowest income categories during the 1970s, students who presumably were given increasing amounts of financial aid. Controlling for family income, Frances found that blacks participated at higher rates than whites did except at the highest income levels. Numerically, however, blacks tended to be clustered at the lower income levels. These data speak to overall rates nationwide, and not to participation rates in different regions or at different types of institutions. Traditionally, many minority and lower-income students have enrolled at community colleges because of their low tuitions, geographical proximity to urban areas, and lower academic requirements. Alterations in policies governing tuition, financial aid, student progress, and the like undoubtedly will affect the distribution of postsecondary students among institutions.

Nontraditional Clienteles

So far, our discussion has centered on the traditional college-age groups because they will continue to contribute the greatest share of postsecondary enrollments. With the aging of the baby-boom generation and the consequent increases in the older age groups, many of these individuals may become recurrent rather than first-time students in the future. To focus attention on potential nontraditional clienteles, it will be useful to review briefly the population dynamics of these older groups.

As the members of the baby boom began to reach age twenty-five, in the early 1970s, the size of the twenty-five- to thirty-four-year-old group began to grow rapidly and has expanded ever since. Likewise, the large group of persons aged forty-five to sixty-four years will begin to expand as the first legion of the baby boom reaches the gates of middle age. Each succeeding decade will first increase, as the baby-boom cohort enters, and then decline sharply, as it passes on and is replaced by the smaller birth cohorts of the 1970s. No age group will subsequently return to the size it attained when it hosted the 1955 to 1964 birth cohort (Spencer, 1984, p. 7). This latter point may be a key one for postsecondary planners who are relying on increases in the adult population to drive future program and enrollment growth (or at least maintenance).

The size of the twenty-five to thirty-four age group is projected to peak by 1990 and subside after that. The group aged thirty-five to forty-four years will peak in 2000, the group aged forty-five to fifty-four will peak in 2010, and so on. Hodgkinson (1983) has likened this demographic movement to that of a mouse through a snake. College enrollments appear to have followed this pattern over the period from 1972 to 1982. More than half the increase in the number of college students was among students twenty-five years old and over. In fact, these increases were stimulated by the number of older women enrolling. Women, however, were most likely to enroll in two-year colleges and in part-time study, thereby signaling a shift away from more traditional college-enrollment patterns (U.S. Bureau of the Census, 1984, p. 2).

These trends suggest, at least in the aggregate, that postsecondary institutions need to develop strategies and program plans to deal with the distension in enrollments caused by the baby boom and its aftershocks. Contraction in postsecondary enrollments is inevitable, but the distribution of enrollments—and marginal additions of new students—will vary across institutional providers and geographical regions of the country. Increased participation by older students may offset the decline in the number of traditional students, but little evidence can be mustered to support the proposition that older students will enroll in the same programs or institutions depleted by the lack of traditional college-age students.

Educational Attainment

Rising levels of educational attainment in the United States may have salutary effects on postsecondary enrollments, but the empirical data to support such an optimistic scenario are limited. The 1980 decennial census, and subsequent current population surveys in 1981 and 1982, depict the levels of educational attainment of the population over the age of twenty-five. These data support the notion of intergenerational gains in levels of educational attainment, wherein younger generations are more educated than older generations. Important regional variations exist, too, with the West and the Midwest having the highest proportions of high school graduates and the South having the lowest.

These statistics do not necessarily represent the productivity of the school systems in each region, because they are influenced by in-migration and out-migration. Thus, the West's share of high school graduates has increased, in part because of the in-migration of young, better-educated individuals over the past fifteen years. The West also leads the other regions in the percentage of its population over age twenty-five who have completed four years of college. Again, overall figures may be misleading: The northeastern population aged twenty-five to thirty-four actually has a higher proportion of college graduates than does the West. The Northeast, however, has a diminishing population base in this highly educated, highly mobile age group (Bruno, 1984, p. 5).

Racial differences in educational attainment are well known and, of course, are not independent of geography. Astin (1982), controlling for age, demonstrated that blacks and Hispanics lag behind whites in their levels of educational attainment. Data from the current population survey for March 1981 show that 86 percent of whites versus 78 percent of blacks twenty-five years of age have completed high school. In contrast, the spread in rates of college attendance for whites and blacks was greater—41 percent versus 32 percent, respectively. Data for younger ages (down to twenty years) suggest that the gap between black and white participation rates may be narrowing, which may serve as evidence of a potential partial offset to declines in numbers of white college students. Data for Hispanics are not so readily available, but one might argue that Hispanics' low rates of postsecondary participation will not increase significantly without substantial programmatic efforts to increase this group's high school completion rates.

Other analyses suggest the potential for a leveling of postsecondary participation rates, which, when superimposed on the receding bulge produced by the baby-boom cohort, foreshadow declining enrollments over the next twenty to fifty years. For men, college enrollment and completion rates of successive cohorts aged twenty-five to twenty-nine peaked in 1976, when more than half of all males born in the years 1947–1951 attended at least one year of college, and more than one-quarter completed four or more years of college. Males born in the years 1952 to 1956 had lower rates of college entrance and completion. These data appear to illustrate the effects of the Vietnam war on college participation rates and support the notion that with increased numbers of minorities represented in each cohort group, college participation may continue to fall unless corrective measures are taken.

A similar analysis of data on the college participation of females aged twenty-five to twenty-nine shows increasing rates of college entry up to the present, but a leveling in rates of college completion (Bruno, 1984, p. 5). These data are consistent with the picture of women participating more in part-time study at two-year institutions than in full-time study leading to the baccalaureate degree. These changing patterns all suggest that it will be virtually impossible to extrapolate postsecondary enrollment trends from past experience or to suggest, in detail, the courses of study that future postsecondary students might pursue. In this environment, individual institutions, having the best knowledge of their own programs and potential student markets, can best assess their own pools of potential clients.

Planning Approaches

I do not mean to suggest that institutional planners and policy makers are totally without resources for assessing their institutional environments and enrollment prospects. In the decades of enrollment growth, demographically inspired market demand forces created enrollment demands, to which institutions responded. Now, however, postsecondary institutions will need to identify clearly at the outset their own respective missions and the clients they wish to serve. Institutional planners will need to develop disaggregated approaches to planning by relating specific programs or enrollment goals to their intended target audiences and assessing the demographic potential of those groups. Because of differences among states and regions, planners will need to develop data bases that are disaggregated by the appropriate demographic and geographical variables. In addition, planners will need to take into account the behaviors of competing institutions, since the future will most probably contain circumscribed numbers of potential clients for most traditional institutions.

Strategic and Operational Analyses

In light of the changing demographic environment, institutional researchers need to focus their analyses on two levels, the first intended to develop overall strategic approaches to defining institutional mission and clientele to be served and the second intended to support specific operational responses that stem from the larger strategies. The analytical techniques employed and the sources of data used may vary according to each of the pursuits, but now more than ever institutional researchers must avoid accepting global generalizations about population trends and must favor a probing specificity.

The differences in approach to assessing the appropriateness of the data used and the level of detail required for each level of analysis may be illustrated by several examples. At the state level, planning studies of potential clienteles may deal with nominal categories: population trends by age, race, and ethnicity, or enrollment trends and market shares by type of institution, geographical area, student characteristics, and the like. These analyses may support statewide or systemwide initiatives and shape widespread political expectations for the behavior of particular institutions or systems. While a certain level of disaggregation is both necessary and desirable for these studies, standard breakdowns often suffice. A study of enrollment trends and forecasts by the California Postsecondary Education Commission (1982) is a good example of this approach.

The commission's report began by reviewing various enrollment projections from the National Center for Education Statistics and other noted analysts to compare and contrast their treatment of impending declines in enrollments. Later chapters discussed the work of California's official demographic agency and its role in enrollment planning and evaluated California's enrollment forecasts. The final chapter attempted to review particular demographic trends, in much the same way as this chapter has attempted to do, in order to sustain top-level attention to planning issues.

To be effective at the campus level, institutional researchers must bring these concerns closer to home and focus on specific clientele groups. This effort may require analyses of demographic data on particular types of individuals from one or more states or regions. In addition to the wealth of cross-sectional data available from the decennial census, state planning or demographic agencies often provide detailed information on intrastate trends. Many of these state agencies are official state contacts for the U.S. Bureau of the Census's state data center program. Each center gets all the data produced for that state by the Census Bureau and agrees to develop a network of affiliates. In turn, some of these state agencies develop local demographic projections.

Institutional researchers need to become better acquainted with census- and state-produced reports and data bases in order to support effective planning. Institutions with sophisticated computing facilities can obtain computer tapes of relevant data directly from the U.S. Bureau of the Census or from their own state data centers to support various demographic analyses. Less technologically sophisticated users will have to rely on printed reports, which often lag behind the data on computer tape by as much as a year or more. (The Census Bureau's Data User Services Division will supply a list of state data centers. See also Riche, 1984d, for a list of state data centers.)

One immediate use of data from the decennial census, is for comparing pertinent characteristics of enrolled students with selected demographic variables of geographical targets: population, age, racial and ethnic mix, income, educational attainment, and other elements. Good examples of census-based approaches are becoming more common as 1980 decennial census figures become available. Nespoli and Radcliffe (1983), using data provided by the regional planning council, the state data center, the county library, the county planning office, and other community colleges, examined the geographical dispersion of Howard Community College (Maryland) students in detail, by census tract and planning district. The study included as key variables the age, race, income, and educational attainment of students. This analysis, when related to the programmatic interests of students, provided a foundation for assessing potential future clienteles on the basis of population trends. The key agenda for institutional researchers following this model will derive from their ability to present alternative scenarios for clientele interests on the basis of alternative programmatic emphases (including the status quo).

This general approach to demographic analysis can be extended easily to the state, regional, or national levels by using data from the decennial census. Since the current population survey deals with a national sample of approximately 60,500, it is not generally feasible to rely on it for disaggregated information. While the U.S. Bureau of the Census is the chief supplier of demographic data for the nation, state data centers and some private agencies also provide key links in the chain of information. Institutional researchers should develop ties with their state data centers in order to take advantage of state specific approaches to census analysis. In addition, many county, regional, or state planning and economic development agencies use demographic information that may be adapted to institutional use.

Data Sources

We have referred repeatedly to data from the 1980 decennial census, the current population survey, and other Census Bureau endeavors. Riche (1984a, 1984b) provides a succinct summary of the types of data and reports available and how to obtain those reports. Monthly issues of *American Demographics* (where these articles by Riche also appear) contain a feature on data sources that serves as a good foundation for neophyte demographers. Several nonprofit organizations also provide data or analyses. The National Planning Association produces its own annual estimates and projections of the population for the United States, four regions, fifty states, and other subdivisions. Riche (1984c, pp. 38-39) describes these reports in detail. The Population Reference Bureau publishes monographs on various topics of national and international concern, many of which pertain to the institutional research and planning concerns discussed in this chapter. While most institutional researchers are familiar with data provided by the National Center for Education Statistics, monitoring current and prospective population shifts may become more important than monitoring previous enrollment trends.

Conclusion

Given the complex demographic changes that the nation is undergoing, planners cannot rely on extrapolation of past trends to predict the future. Institutional researchers, using more speculative simulations and questions, should develop alternative assumptions about potential clienteles by analyzing specifically developed demographic and related data. Analysis should differentiate among local, state, regional, and national trends and should acknowledge the possible effects of public policy decisions on enrollment preferences.

Projecting demand for postsecondary education goes beyond analysis of changes in demography and far beyond historical trend analysis. As this chapter has tried to show, however, an appreciation of demographic trends related to postsecondary education in the post-baby-boom era is a prerequisite to good planning. This chapter began by saying that the relationship of postsecondary institutions to their environments should be characterized by responsiveness to the effects of population growth and increasing demand. How postsecondary institutions will fare in the future will depend on their ability to forecast their willingness to serve new clienteles.

References

Astin, A. W. *Minorities in Higher Education.* San Francisco: Jossey-Bass, 1982.

Bruno, R. R. *Educational Attainment in the United States: March 1981 and 1980.* Current Population Reports, Series P-20, no. 390. Washington, D.C.: U.S. Department of Commerce, Bureau of the Census, 1984.

California Postsecondary Education Commission. *Trends in Higher Education Enrollment: A Report on Enrollment Projections, Management, and Development by the Staff of the California Postsecondary Education Commission.* Sacramento: California Postsecondary Education Commission, 1982.

Dolman, G., Jr., and Kaufman, N. S. *Minorities in Higher Education: The Changing Southwest—Texas.* Boulder, Colo.: Western Interstate Commission for Higher Education, 1984.

Fishlow, H. *A Demographic Overview of Postsecondary Education.* Washington, D.C.: National Commission on Student Financial Assistance, 1982.

Frances, C. *Basic Facts on College-Going Rates by Income, Race, Sex, and Age, 1970 to 1980.* Washington, D.C.: National Commission on Student Financial Assistance, 1982.

Grant, W. V., and Snyder, T. D. *Digest of Education Statistics, 1983–84.* Washington, D.C.: U.S. Government Printing Office, 1984.

Hodgkinson, H. *Guess Who's Coming to College: Your Students in 1990.* Washington, D.C.: National Association of Independent Colleges and Universities, 1983.

McConnell, W. R., and Kaufman, N. S. *High School Graduates: Projections for the Fifty States (1982–2000).* Boulder, Colo.: Western Interstate Commission for Higher Education, 1984.

Nespoli, L. A., and Radcliffe, S. K. *Census Analysis: A Look at HCC Credit Students Based on the 1980 Census.* Research Report Number 30. Columbia, Md.: Office of Research and Planning, Howard Community College, 1983.

Regents of the State of New York. *The Regents' Tentative Statewide Plan for the Development of Postsecondary Education in New York State, 1984.* Albany: The University of the State of New York, 1984.

Riche, M. F. "1980 Census Data Products." *American Demographics,* August 1984a, pp. 32–35.

Riche, M. F. "The Non-Census Census Bureau." *American Demographics,* September 1984b, pp. 38–39.

Riche, M. F. "The NPA." *American Demographics,* July 1984c, pp. 38–39.

Riche, M. F. "The State of the States' State Data Centers." *American Demographics,* October 1984d, pp. 28–33.

Spencer, G. *Projections of the Population of the United States, by Age, Sex, and Race: 1983 to 2080.* Current Population Reports, Series P-25, no. 952. Washington, D.C.: U.S. Department of Commerce, Bureau of the Census, 1984.

U.S. Bureau of the Census. *School Enrollment—Social and Economic Characteristics of Students: October 1982 (Advance Report).* Current Population Reports, Series P-20, no. 392. Washington, D.C.: U.S. Department of Commerce, Bureau of the Census, 1984.

Norman S. Kaufman is director of institutional studies and analysis and of academic planning at the State University of New York at Binghamton. He came to his current position in 1984 from the Western Interstate Commission for Higher Education, where he was responsible for a number of comparative studies of education in the thirteen western states and the nation as a whole.

This chapter records a discussion among several experts on assessing the economic environment of higher education.

Economics and Educational Planning

Larry Leslie, Russell Rumberger, William H. Pickens, Patrick M. Callan, Keith G. Pailthorp

Pat Callan: Any book on the subject of how colleges and universities should scan the environment for purposes of institutional planning needs to consider how higher education planners and policy makers who are concerned about long-term trends should think about what is known about the economy.

When we planned this volume, we considered asking a single economist to write on this topic, but we came to the conclusion that having one individual offer opinions on this topic would not be very useful. It would also put a considerable burden on the person to try to represent the range of current thinking about financial and economic issues and trends in higher education and planning.

We decided that a dialogue involving several economists would raise the appropriate issues better, and so we brought together Larry Leslie of the University of Arizona, Russell Rumberger of Stanford, and Bill Pickens of the California Postsecondary Education Commission to discuss several issues concerning scanning the economic environment of colleges and universities. Our overarching questions are:

P. M. Callan (ed.). *Environmental Scanning for Strategic Leadership.*
New Directions for Institutional Research, no. 52. San Francisco: Jossey-Bass, Winter 1986.

1. What factors in the economic environment are important if you are trying to understand the environment for college and university planning?
2. What economic indices, trends, and considerations should institutional researchers monitor and rely on for planning?
3. What kinds of assumptions about the economic outlook for higher education should you make, knowing that assumptions about the near future will need to be altered or revised as time goes on?

For example, in terms of factors to watch out for, governmental and political actions are clearly important because they affect state and federal revenues and thus the financing of higher education, particularly public education. When you think of what happened in the last seven years in California, after Proposition 13, you sense that these influences probably have been as important as anything else that has happened in the environment of California's public colleges and universities over this decade.

Keith Pailthorp: The bridge that we are trying to build in this book is that from the institutional researcher to the chief executive officer and the governing board of the institution. Institutional researchers need to do their work so that it contributes to wise decisions by institutional leaders. They need to make environmental information comprehensible to policy makers on the campus.

Russell Rumberger: That linkage definitely has to be made to state activities, especially if you are in a public institution, but no institution—private or public—operates in a vacuum. All institutions are parts of systems, and they have to be aware of what their fellow institutions are doing, as well as what is happening at state, national, and international levels.

Elements in the Environment

Larry Leslie: As an example, I've been told that the Pentagon is planning to begin to farm out their educational work to colleges and universities and other organizations over the next several years. That's the kind of thing an environmental scanning system ought to pick up, at least at those institutions located near military bases.

Bill Pickens: One of the things I'm most interested in are the indices of trends that institutional leaders need to consider. One of the things most economists have not done, except for those who get interested in the stock market, is to try to identify a set of indices—even very simple ones—that, through extrapolation or other mathematical manipulation, may help predict the future. We're trying to do that at the state level in California by developing between six and ten indices that try to show trends in institutional funding. One shows the proportion of state general funds and property-tax revenues that have gone over the past decade to public higher education in the state. From this, we can identify those years and conditions that changed the proportion significantly. We also have an instructional ratio index that indicates the proportion of total institutional expenditures represented by instruction. This index shows that instruction is declining steadily in the four-year institutions as a percent of their total budgets.

If I were an institutional planner interested in indices or trends that show fundamental changes in the environment, what would those be? It seems to me that we ought to be able to identify for institutional researchers five or six crucial ratios or trends that they should watch out for. For example, according to *The Chronicle of Higher Education,* faculty salaries are catching up with inflation. They're up by 6.7 percent for all faculty and 7.1 percent for continuing faculty. That's well over 2 percent higher than the inflation rate, and it's the largest real increase since the 1960s. The question is, what is the relationship between faculty salaries and inflation? Is it a lag relationship? In other words, during low periods of inflation, do faculty salaries tend to outpace inflation, and vice versa?

Leslie: There's some evidence that the recent inflationary period and the period of relatively declining resources in higher education were overall moneymakers for institutions because institutions were able to keep salary increases well below inflation and thus wound up with more discretionary money than they would have had otherwise. It appears that the gap between salaries and inflation is what we have used to pay for the growth in higher education expenditures over the last dozen years or so.

Pickens: Certainly during the 1970s, and at least until the real bad times in 1981, institutional revenues as a whole actually increased in terms of FTE. Yet exactly at that time, *Academe* claims, faculty salary purchasing power was falling behind by some 20 percent.

Rumberger: It seems to me that you would need key indicators of many aspects of institutional operations in order to construct a planning outlook—salaries, enrollments, characteristics of students, and the like, plus salaries relative to those offered by business and industry. High salaries in the private sector can attract faculty away from institutions, as illustrated in fields such as engineering, so that although engineering enrollments are up,institutions lack the faculty to teach the new students. I agree that we can think of charting indicators, but there are a lot of them.

Leslie: The body of literature that comes to mind here is what I would call the "indicators" literature, such as the measures developed by Howard Bowen and John Minter. One part of this literature has never been disseminated very well—the work NCHEMS was doing several years ago. They hired a half-dozen of us to build some indices and calculate trend lines as far back as we could go. Mike Tierney participated in this effort, they had a couple of their own staff people participate, and the rest of us were involved in developing other indicators. The data had limitations, but the ones I know best—the ones I constructed, on student costs—have been very helpful in answering various policy questions.

Rumberger: Is NCHEMS retaining these indices now on an ongoing basis?

Leslie: I don't know, but the idea was that they would be continued. If NCHEMS is doing so, that would certainly be worthwhile. Certainly some "accepted truths" about financial trends were undermined by Mike Tierney's research, and some of the trends I found were surprising to me. They speak very directly to the national debate right now between Reagan and Congress over student aid.

Economic Forecasts and Forecasting

Callan: I think there is an even earlier question that we should address—the question of the use by institutional researchers and planners of existing economic forecasts, since a lot of people have produced forecasts that have been wrong. Do the incorrect economic forecasts mean we would be better off advising institutional planners and policy makers just to ignore them and instead simply extrapolate from past trends?

Rumberger: My advice would be not to rely on any single economic forecast but instead look at ranges. If you read the Council of Economic Advisers or the Reagan administration or the Congressional Budget Office, you'll see conflict between the administration's and CBO's forecasting.

I would include the worst-case scenarios, and I'd show all of the different ones and say, "It looks like some people are assuming a 1 or 2 percent real-growth rate, while others are going for 3 percent." Economists' ability to forecast the scope of the last recession over the last four years—its significance, how bad it was going to be, when it was going to bottom out, how much growth would occur afterwards—was very dismal.

My own unsubstantiated view is that we're in a much more volatile period economically than usual. We are subjected to wild swings, such as the four recessions from 1969 on, with the last one being the worst. So I think that if the past and present are indicative of anything, it is that we will be subjected to more fluctuations in our economy in the near future.

Leslie: That strikes me as a good warning. I would throw in as an amendment to what you say that for so much of what we are dealing with in forecasting, there simply are no precedents. For example, the biggest factor in the American economy today, at least if you believe the mass media, is our federal deficit. But we don't have any prior experience with $200 billion deficits.

Rumberger: The administration has certainly changed its views about it since Reagan's 1980 statement that it was not going to have a deficit, because deficits were bad, and therefore the budget would be balanced by 1984. But in the last few years, deficits have gained acceptance, at least in the current administration: They really are not that bad, and we can still have economic growth. It's mostly that economists, and especially traditional economists, have been saying it's really bad and it's going to be a problem. I think that a lot of the analyses that appear in the press are pretty simplistic about the deficit, other than noting it has an effect on interest rates. But I think you're right: We don't know the consequences of so large a deficit.

My other reason for predicting greater instability would be the internationalization of our economy. That is, in the future we will be more subjected to the global economy, as every other nation's economy will be. There is more competition among nations, and as a result there's more threat of influence from international sources on the goods market, the services market, the financial market, and the labor market. The internationalization of the global economy points to more interdependency among economies, including the debt problems of the underdeveloped countries and the increasing gap between developing countries and developed countries. We know that trade has increased worldwide, but we don't know how this increase affects any one economy, and in what ways.

Pailthorp: Could this international interdependence prove to be a kind of insurance policy in that if one part of your trade market goes bad, you would still have some others to depend on? It seems to me that you're saying that's a possibility, because of increased and heightened interdependence between all economies.

Rumberger: I think so. Look at the last recession: It hit lots of countries differently, and I'm not sure why. We just didn't all experience the same recession.

Leslie: We've pulled each other out together, though.

Rumberger: Yes, except that we've all been pulled out in different ways. Most countries still have very high unemployment, and they look at us and say, "You have solved your own problem. What about us?" We have much less economic information on the international level than we have on the United States. We don't know much about other countries individually, nor about the interrelationships among countries.

Another trend that's occurring is the way technology is reshaping the whole marketplace. It's illustrated by GM's "Saturn" car, which we're going to design in the United States but which will be a world car in that its components are going to be produced internationally and it's going to be marketed worldwide. Companies like General Motors are realizing that we are in an international environment and that we are going to do things differently. We're going to have to change our mentality of how our economy operates in that it isn't any longer freestanding. Our domestic economy has ties and influences to other economies, just like each of our states. States can't operate in isolation. They have to worry about what other states are doing in competing among each other for business. But now their competition is really on an international scale. A city or state can lose a manufacturing plant to Taiwan as easily as to Texas.

I see a lot of unpredictability for this reason, in terms of more competition locally, regionally, nationally, and internationally. That's part of the rallying cry for improving the educational system. Today, you don't have to be a technically advanced country to make cars or build steel plants or assemble integrated circuits. In the past, only the United States could do these kinds of sophisticated things. But today, Malaysia and Taiwan can produce integrated circuits and very sophisticated computers. And it's not that the Taiwanese are taking away our markets: It's U.S. firms invested in Taiwan who are doing it.

I think that all of this is fundamentally different than it has been in the past. Now we're talking about a marketplace where virtually anything can be produced anywhere by anyone. The only thing that's still left for the United States is leading-edge developments like the supercomputer.

Pickens: It really raises two problems for higher education, I think. The first is to try to make some reasonable prediction about the resources that will flow to higher education. But the second, and in a way the more important one, is how we should educate students in order to prepare them to deal with that kind of uncertainty.

Leslie: If I were to suggest what the changes in the national and world economy mean for higher education, I'd counsel that as planners we not get too carried away with the trends of the moment. In the early 1970s, we heard much talk about the "steady state" and the coming decline in higher education, and everyone seemed to accept it on faith after hearing about it a few times. When Howard Miller and I set out to write the monograph called "Higher Education and the Steady State" that was published by ERIC and AAHE in 1974, we started out accepting the decline on faith; but as we started digging around in the literature, particularly in biology and in economics, we soon discovered that all was not ringing true. By the time we finished, we realized that we had been caught up in untested assumptions. We wound up concluding that almost everybody had been far too pessimistic in their estimates of the enrollment future.

We all get caught up in this sort of thinking every time there is a bear or a bull market. The temptation is to think that the trends are going to last forever. I think there's a lot of that kind of reaction to the deficit. Maybe the deficit is going to be around forever at about $200 billion, and maybe it isn't. I don't know. But we make guesses about how much money in marginal terms is going to be available to higher education for the next ten or twenty years, based on such assumptions.

A few months ago, Clark Kerr was quoted to the effect that the states were going to be playing a larger role in financing higher education. So far, he appears to be fundamentally correct; but at the same time it is difficult to foresee a lesser long-term federal role as international markets are becoming more competitive. With Korea, Malaysia, Taiwan, and the European Common Market competing strongly for our international markets, it seems to me that education takes on added importance, particularly in technical areas, and that a greater federal role is likely in the long run.

This gets you into thinking about the role of higher education in a postindustrial society, and if you take Russ's idea of the ranges of economic forecasts and ask about the worst case, does it necessarily follow that higher education is going to be a depressed industry? The states that have had the toughest times economically are the ones that are now putting more of their marginal money selectively into higher education in an effort to promote "high tech."

Pickens: But, Larry, wouldn't you agree that one of the reasons why we have had stability rather than a downturn in enrollments is that college and university planners were well alerted to the forthcoming downturn in the college-age population?

For instance, one of the things that's quite clear in California is that we've had a declining high school graduation rate and a rapidly growing Hispanic population. Thus, for at least ten years, the University of California in particular has made extra efforts to recruit Hispanic students. The community colleges have of course done so for twenty years.

Leslie: I agree, and federal student aid came about for that very reason. But all is not always as it may seem. About 1969 or 1970, you'll recall, we were worried about saving private higher education. The Committee for Economic Development's task force on the management and financing of colleges was established for that purpose. The CED recommended need-based student aid, but its motive was not more equitable distribution of wealth; it was to save the private institutions that were in bad shape at that time.

Pickens: Using your case of enrollment decline, it seems to me that what planning has to do is to show current trends and say, "If these trends continue along certain levels of magnitude, the following will result." There will obviously be midcourse corrections. Those are made all the time. But what planning does, presumably, is to lay out the current trends of the most important independent variables and ask, "Do you want this to result? If not, then here are possible policy or fiscal tools to avoid it."

Leslie: There is a whole body of literature that is extraordinarily useful in figuring that out. Howard Miller and I didn't get our own thinking straightened away until we read Joseph Schumpeters's theory of the firm under stress in his *Theory of Economic Development,* and until Howard, who is a biologist, brought in material from research on biological "climax communities." Such theories really got us to thinking about what institutions, as firms, are likely to do when they get into trouble. What's happening today illustrates these theories nicely: Colleges adapt. There are, for example, few liberal arts colleges in America any more. The exceptions are about twenty elite institutions. All the rest are comprehensive colleges that are offering professional career programs to survive.

Economic Development and Higher Education

Rumberger: I sense that we are answering this question in two ways: What are the implications of some economic future, good or bad or somewhere in between, for higher education revenues, student financial aid, and the rest? And what should the role of higher education be in improving economic development? Every time I give a talk about the latter topic, I always qualify it by saying, "Of course, we really all know the other things that higher education is supposed to be doing besides worrying about economic development"—you know, improving people's cultural heritage and political participation and whatever. But then I divide the answer into two parts: the role of higher education in preparing students for the work world, and its role in the whole R&D effort. At Stanford, we see much of the latter going on through alliances with business and industry and the establishing of centers and institutes and laboratories and the like. Texas is big on it, too, as is MIT.

In some ways, I think, colleges and universities are seeing themselves as having a more important role in economic development. That's the strategy that a lot of localities are using, too: "O.K., let's make sure we form these alliances between higher education and the business community and the elementary and secondary schools, so that educators know what business needs. Then we will provide trained students in these technical fields." When you ask yourself why we are seeing so much of this now, as compared to ten or fifteen years ago, I think part of the answer is a realization on the part of the business community that higher education really is an asset in that it's where our ideas and livelihoods for the future are going to come from. But part of it, from the institution's point of view, is that it's for institutional survival. Revenues have been tough to come by. We need new sources of income and support for students, so we'll go out and embrace the business community.

Callan: Is there some danger of overselling this? We've gone through cycles before when, whatever the society was looking for, we said we had it—whether it was winning the Cold War, taking care of the cities, or whatever—and the failure to live up to that promise was followed by a period of disillusionment. Certainly every state and every institution that I know of is out to become the high-tech capital of the world, and they can't all be.

Rumberger: Certainly there won't be more than a half-dozen high-tech centers in the country, despite every university's hopes. In addition, one region's gain will be another's loss. Attracting new businesses may be a great strategy for particular states or localities; but nationally, I don't think we'll be any better off. Relocating high-tech firms from California to Arizona may help Arizona, but it doesn't help the country a great deal, and we may simply be developing a breed of carpetbagger corporation that picks up and moves to the highest bidder.

Pressed to their limit, these partnerships between industry and the university raise basic questions of academic freedom and governance. For instance, we've had a debate at Stanford over who should appoint the members of a new research institute. A corporation wanted to have direct influence over who was going to be hired, yet these people were going to be called faculty members. The corporation challenged our notion of academic governance, but we said, "Hey, wait a second; academics have to choose who their academic colleagues are to be and not have a company say that it wants this person or that person." In that respect, I think there can be dangers.

In general, I think the reaction of higher education institutions like Stanford is that we can deal with such issues and safeguard institutional freedoms. Our President Kennedy was a big spokesman for this in our biotechnology center and our new integrated-circuit center. In these centers, companies can send in their employees who work on projects as fellows, side by side with faculty. They can take the research findings back to their companies and apply them to their products, but the research is public, rather than private.

Leslie: Given all this, it seems to me that the connection between higher education and economic growth must increase. I recall Denison's work of a decade or more ago (and that continues still), showing that over a thirty-year period, 20 percent of the growth of our national income could be attributed directly to education and 23 percent to the advancement of knowledge and a reduced lag between knowledge development and its implementation. More recent work shows that the contribution of education to the economy declined only modestly from the 1960s to the 1980s. I also remember some OECD work that tried to separate out investment in human capital from physical capital in explaining gross national product or national income growth. One of the conclusions of that work was that when you try to explain variations in national income growth rates among developing countries, it is investment in people—that is, in education—more than investment in physical capital that largely accounts for the differences. In his book on international rates of return, Psacharopoulos showed this about as well as anyone.

Pickens: But one of the problems of dealing with higher education in terms of economic growth is that it has two major contributions that are distinct and presumably could be undertaken by different institutions. One is the research aspect. The other is the labor training aspect. To mix those two together and come up with some residual aspect, as the typical reviews of economics do, is very, very difficult.

Russ, you mentioned some of the issues that arise in research with regard to academic freedom and governance. There is, as you know, an equally hot debate going on in vocational education around the nation about whether educational institutions should in effect be just job-training agencies, responsive to business in the way that the whole world of proprietary institutions is.

Most of the vocational people I've talked with, both in the adult schools and community colleges, are absolutely adamant about the need to teach broad-based skills in vocational training. What do you think about that as a labor market trend? Which way is higher education going to go?

Leslie: Whenever I get into a discussion like this, I remember the revelation of several years ago that businesses recruit people who are broadly educated but hire people who are narrowly trained.

Rumberger: I think there is some change going on here because of the tendency of government, as part of the regional development competition we were talking about earlier, to promise companies a lot, not just in terms of tax incentives, free land, and other subsidies, but also education, in terms of promising to offer more of the job-specific or firm-specific short-term training that you mention. I think the other thing that is a bit different now is that it's a tight market for many institutions, both because of the declining pool of young people and because of the economic squeeze so many places are in. So whatever they can do to maintain the economic base, they'll do. Some of them will offer anything that people will sign up for, whether it's job-specific, general education, or whatever. I think there's a marketing aspect to it: "What's our market? What can we offer this market that will sell?"

Leslie: In terms of long-term indicators, scanning could reveal whether or not companies and other types of institutions are getting into our business, and to what extent we're getting into their business. Community colleges in particular find no trouble at all justifying job-specific programs, paid for by the public, as a way to attract industries to their communities, and I can imagine that they'll be the first to take advantage of the defense department's beginning to contract with institutions to do their training.

Rumberger: One problem here is that we don't know how much training actually goes on in businesses. There have been some studies done trying to get a handle on it, but in terms of trends, we have nothing. So it's real hard to say anything about it.

Leslie: If scanning is your responsibility, you may not have hard data, but you can at least highlight issues such as these we're discussing, walk around them, see what they look like, and maybe poke a stick at them. You don't necessarily have to have the answer in order to pose the question.

Rumberger: Certainly one issue that's involved here is the whole notion of whom we're training students for. Are we training them for themselves, which is their thirty- to forty- to fifty-year working span—preparing them in what we think is best for them over their careers? Or are we training them for what is best for the companies, which can be very short-term?

We have to be careful, when we talk about occupational trends, to remember that what employers need today is probably not what they will need tomorrow. Computers are transforming many fields to the point where people will be doing different things from these jobs involved in the past. IBM is hiring more liberal arts graduates and fewer engineers. Their argument is that today's technology allows anybody to design a circuit or do other kinds of engineering tasks, but they need thinkers, creative people, people who have a broader vision to operate in a changing world. Stanford has just implemented a bachelor of science in engineering degree—not electrical engineering or mechanical engineering, but plain old engineering. It has reduced the engineering requirements and increased nonengineering courses in order to prepare a more generally educated engineer.

One of the implications I see in the internationalization of the economy and the increased mobility of capital is that it means considerably less stability of firms. They can relocate to your backyard tomorrow and then all too soon be gone. There are dangers under these conditions in being too responsive to the immediate needs of business by training students for specific jobs. You can say, "Well, it's the students' fault, because they should make their own assessments of the value of immediate placement in a job or of learning something that will help them in the long run." But I think we have more responsibility to students than that—if only to the point of providing counseling that explains to them, "We have these kinds of programs that are oriented to the immediate needs of this or that firm, and we can foresee likely placements in these areas. But if you want a fundamental education that will serve you your lifetime or more general preparation that will give you the background to pursue specific training later, either in this institution or somewhere else, then you should consider another program."

In terms of institutional planning, the caution to institutions creating programs to serve the needs of a specific business is that your program may not be around for very long because the firm may not be nearby for very long.

Leslie: And I'd add: Don't tenure your faculty.

Rumberger: You're right. It's easy to start new programs, but it's a lot harder to stop them. And it affects your five- or ten-year budgeting and planning, because programs aimed at meeting short-term needs are subject to abrupt shifts, so you can't plan faculty and physical resources—like laboratories, shops, and clinical facilities—for them.

One implication of this in terms of planning, it seems to me, is to think through, before adding something, how to phase it down and even out, if necessary, after you phase it in. And then you decide what to do about faculty and tenure and equipment and facilities and things like that.

Leslie: This relates to the extraordinary sensitivity of students to changing labor market conditions. For example, just a year ago we were hearing that no science and mathematics teachers could be found. Last year, Arizona's two major public universities produced only three graduates in mathematics education between them. This year, my university started a new math-science teacher education program, and we have forty students in it already. When students read about areas of high employment demand, they react. They react so well that high-demand fields can quickly become saturated. Many of the allied health professions have become supersaturated; all of a sudden we have a glut of MBAs; and of course everybody knows about law.

Long-Term Perspectives and Trends

Pailthorp: But what are the incentives for a planner or institutional research officer, given the turnover in presidents and the often short tenure of other administrators and staff, to take a long-term perspective like that in planning? If you were a president, why not hire a lot of part-time faculty to teach these courses at $800 or $1,000 each, so if the program folds, you're only back where you started. Are there any incentives for the institution to take the long-term perspective, from an economic standpoint?

Leslie: The community colleges, I think, have gotten themselves in trouble in this regard because they've been taking a short-term view and have lost a lot of what was once called "community." There are some good trend-line figures around on the proportion of faculty who are part-time employees. It's amazing how this percentage has grown in the last twenty years.

Pailthorp: Whom are they in trouble with? Their main sources of income?

Leslie: Yes. They have shown to their benefactors—either legislatures or local taxpayers—that they can offer so-called higher education at a low cost by hiring what I call itinerant faculty members at low wages, so now they're stuck with a financing system that forces them to produce student credit hours at unreasonably low cost. In order to continue to generate the same number of credit hours at the same cost, they've got to continue to use these adjunct faculty.

Pickens: The way California is handling this problem is by losing 20 percent of its community college enrollment.

Rumberger: I think even more of this short-term mentality pervades business in the United States. It's immediate cash and profit versus long-range planning and long-term growth, stability, and morale. One of the things observers of American business talk about is its emphasis on short-term profit. We set up business; we declare bankruptcy; we dissolve the business; and we start another firm. Some educational institutions suffer from it, too. Not the Stanfords, the Berkeleys, and other long-established institutions, perhaps, but some of the more marginal and younger ones.

Callan: Russ, it seems to me that one of the reactions that institutional research officers and planners may have to these large issues that we've been talking about is a sense of paralysis. I mean by that, there's a tendency, what with the increased sophistication of knowledge and data that are available, for us to say to ourselves, "Why even bother to think about this stuff, since the future's so unpredictable?" And there's also a tendency to believe that factors in the environment will have an impact on other institutions, but not on our own. So it seems to me that we need to ask whether there are some handles that people ought to latch on to—trends or factors or indices that they should watch systematically and continuously, so that those who want to take account of all the possible information can sort through it and find the most important in terms of the future of their institution.

Leslie: I think so. In higher education planning, one can easily become overwhelmed with too much data. It is also tempting to get caught up in a particular trend, when in fact it is a very small part of the total picture. Our fixation with "high-tech" seems a classic illustration of this tendency, since you, Russ, and Henry Levin have illustrated that the number of such future jobs will be considerably smaller than many believe.

In the worst case, we may just give up and hang in there, grinding out our annual reports and annual enrollment forecasts, knowing that by the time we get all the required reports written, we will have no time left for important work.

Callan: Isn't that last possibility largely a function of the expectations of the leadership of the institution? If scanning is seen as part of what's needed to exercise leadership in the institution, then presidents, vice-presidents, and deans will make use of it and encourage it. But if it's seen as a technical, insulated function, like producing compliance reports, it won't get done.

Rumberger: I agree. If we want to scan, but need to focus on a few important indices, I'd probably divide them into two types—those that monitor the external environment of the institution and those that monitor its internal environment. Obviously, they're related, but you look outside your institution for one and inside for the other.

Leslie: Among your external factors would be population trends, wouldn't they—such as the age and minority mix of your area's population. Business-cycle data would be another. Changes in costs of attendance would be a third. If you're a public institution, changes in the tax base would also be important.

Rumberger: In terms of the external environment, wherever you have sources of revenue or potential sources of revenue, you'll want to monitor them. Anything that affects your revenues—whatever those sources are—you'll want to categorize them and develop indices related to them.

Leslie: Earlier, Bill, you noted a basic one for public institutions: the share of the state budget that higher education is getting. A second is your own institution's share of the higher education share. And a broad related area that you'd want to scan is the tax structure, including tax incentives, tax deductions, tax credits, and tax savings plans for students. You should also be concerned about revenue diversity or revenue mix. That is, institutions need to be careful they don't become overly dependent on any one source of revenue, whether tuition or annual state appropriations.

You'd probably also want to look at effects of price on student demand. Steven Hoenack and W. L. Weiler at the University of Minnesota have constructed some models, which include a dozen or more variables that are constantly scanned in composing annual projections. That's what you have to do in the enrollment planning business, and enrollment planning is still pretty fundamental to financial planning. This reminds me, however, of an important caveat. Nationally, since 1977, the marginal revenue in state appropriations per student has represented only about two-tenths of the average cost of education. In other words, only if your marginal costs are less than two-tenths of your average costs are you going to receive more dollars for additional enrollments than you have to spend. I doubt that any institution has marginal costs that low. Thus, enrollment increases across the country in the past eight or nine years have on average been money-losing propositions, yet institutions are still acting as though enrollment growth is going to save their bacon.

State and federal student aid is another thing that you have to keep track of. We've developed a pattern in higher education of constantly increasing tuition prices—in the last few years, at a rate a good deal faster than inflation. Through financial aid, we've been able to offset this increase to some extent for low-income students. But what happens when you put the brakes on financial aid, or even make substantial cuts in it? You're not going to be able to cut tuition prices, because institutions have come to depend on the revenue. What will be the effect on demand, particularly in the lower-status private institutions? It's those institutions that are most dependent on student aid. I estimated some years ago that something like 20 or 25 percent of their enrollments depended on this aid. These are the institutions that student aid clearly has done a good job in salvaging, thus contributing to student choice of institutions. My sense of the empirical research, however, is that student aid hasn't done much for overall access, and it's done even less for student retention and completion of programs. I've argued for ten years that states and the federal government ought to do a better job of monitoring the effects of student aid, so that a better-informed student aid policy can emerge.

Rumberger: In terms of relative prices, isn't it true that the expensive institutions get together, and that a fair number of them agree on setting their prices within certain limits?

Leslie: Absolutely right. I think it's clear that they get together annually to discuss tuition pricing. The antitrust folks ought to get after them.

Rumberger: Among private institutions that depend on alumni contributions, alumni income levels would be particularly interesting. Some places are making files on alumni, and they probably survey at least a sample of alumni about their income. Some of the professional schools, like our business school and law school, rely heavily on those files to target gift giving. I wouldn't be surprised to find salary information in those files.

Leslie: Alumni offices keep pretty good records about their donor behavior, particularly in the private institutions. They can given Madison Avenue a lot of lessons about p.r. Even the public institutions are becoming more savvy, since such gifts represent the extra money that allows them to do the special things regular revenues do not fund.

We've already touched on another important matter—the emerging occupational trends and industrial manpower needs that might lead to new academic programs. Here, you would need to rely on such sources as industry projections and trends in your area, whether a local community for a community college, or a region for a state university. Almost anywhere you are located, you can find a bureau of economic research or chamber of commerce that keeps track of new companies coming into town, the job classifications of people hired, and that sort of thing.

Rumberger: The work that Henry Levin, myself, and others have done, pointing to the big growth in the service sector of the labor market, is important here—for example, my book *Overeducation in the U.S. Labor Market,* published by Praeger in 1981. If it's true that the growth is not going to be in high technology, but instead in McDonald's stands, hotels, and other services, this has implications for higher education. I would think that institutions would want to know how successful their different programs are, in order to ask if there are any programs they should phase out or consolidate.

Leslie: We've talked a good deal about job training, but we shouldn't forget the impact of culture and taste on higher education. When we try to explain why enrollments have not declined as prices have gone up, the biggest factor is changes in the culture—particularly vis-à-vis women and minorities. In other words, individual tastes or preferences have changed. There is a greater "taste" for higher education today. Part of the reason for this is that as we educate more and more people in higher education, we create greater parental expectations for the education of their children. If parents have attended college, their children are likely to do so as well. So the propensity to consume higher education naturally increases and, further, may compound over time. As you probably know, adult women have largely sustained enrollment levels in recent years—not traditional college-age women, but adult women returning to work. This trend is reflected in the increase of women's participation in the labor market.

We shouldn't forget the older population, either. I know that the traditional human-capital view would suggest that this group is never going to be large, because employment time is not sufficient to provide adequate economic payoff. But we are beginning to see that with people retiring earlier, and with tastes changing, older people are in fact beginning to enroll in larger and larger numbers simply for personal satisfaction. This is a tremendously large pool that will grow dramatically in the years ahead, and just a couple of percentage points' increase in the participation rate of this pool would add significantly to higher education enrollments nationally.

Rumberger: Institutions clearly are marketing themselves to this pool through their summer conferences and part learning-part vacation programs.

Pailthorp: To what extent will the shortened work week, higher per-capita income, greater disposable income, and other changes affect this potential?

Rumberger: I don't know if it will be a big percentage increase; but as you say, it won't take much of a percentage increase to increase the numbers. Institutions can make these programs quite attractive. They can think about who their clients are and whom they're trying to sell their services to. And whomever they see themselves serving, they should chart the changes relating to these groups. If you're going to target more of your enrollments to older people, then you would want to chart the percentage of older people in your community.

Leslie: Don't forget early retirement. Among people who are forty-five, fifty, fifty-five years old, there is a lot of accumulated wealth, because they accumulated assets before the recent burst of inflation. My old friends at Penn State have bought their farms, and their wives are on the faculty.

The budgetary implications of a potentially younger faculty are important. We know that we'll be getting a younger faculty soon, regardless of the extent of early retirement. If early retirements occur in large numbers, we're going to have a compound effect, and the "youthing" of the faculty is going to come earlier. In Arizona, we have an early retirement incentive program that was quickly "oversubscribed." About twice as many people wanted to take advantage of it as had been expected. So certainly it's something to keep an eye on.

Rumberger: And not only retirement, but semiretirement—going on half-time status.

Leslie: That's right. We allow faculty to continue to work at the university at 49 percent of their salaries, and it's extremely popular. You can continue your teaching but also run a real estate business. We should keep an eye on that as well.

I guess the basic issue we're discussing here is faculty flow. Retirement is only one part of the issue. Every institution ought to have a faculty-flow model that covers not only age but also tenure status by department and net flow every year, in terms of people leaving and deaths and other changes. It's essential for planning.

Rumberger: We've moved into indices of the internal institutional environment with your faculty-flow model. We could add facilities, space utilization, maintenance, and other institutional trends. Land use might be one of them. Stanford does a lot of long-term land-use planning, because it has so much land. And we could include nonfaculty staffing. In Stanford's case, what business and industry in Silicon Valley pay their employees is important to us, because it affects our ability to attract staff. Housing prices are important, too.

Pat, earlier you asked about sources of economic information. As I see it, they range all the way from publications through computerized data bases to personal networks of colleagues. The most accessible, it seems to me, are publications such as those from the U.S. Bureau of the Census, where you can get regional and national information. Among the national data bases are "Source," "Dialogue," and "Composure." Even *The Chronicle of Higher Education* has its own data base that an institutional research staff can use.

Callan: And, Russ, I gather from our discussion that these sources of information won't necessarily be the same for all of higher education. After listening to all of you, I guess I'd conclude that, depending on your institution and location, the issues for scanning won't be the same, the answers won't be the same, the indices won't be, and these sources shouldn't be, either. However, I leave this discussion increasingly convinced of the need for institutional planners to look beyond the campus and beyond the next year in trying to inform and educate the leadership of their institutions.

Larry Leslie is professor of higher education and director of the Center for the Study of Higher Education, University of Arizona.

Russell Rumberger is an economist and a senior research associate in the School of Education, Stanford University. He has written extensively on education and labor markets, and most recently with Henry Levin, on the educational implications of high technology.

William H. Pickens assumed the executive directorship of the California Postsecondary Education Commission in August 1986, where formerly he was director of fiscal analysis with responsibilities for following all fiscal legislation affecting postsecondary institutions in California.

Patrick M. Callan is vice-president of the Education Commission of the States. Until mid-1986 he was director of the California Postsecondary Education Commission, California's coordinating council for education beyond high school.

Keith G. Pailthorp is assistant director for planning and a postsecondary education administrator at the California Postsecondary Education Commission, where he has directed the commission's long-range planning project, "A Prospectus for California Postsecondary Education, 1985–2000."

Institutional researchers can provide useful and appropriate data on institutional financial change by following three general guidelines for financial trend analysis.

Funding over Time: Measuring Institutional Finance

William H. Pickens

No planning effort would be credible without some attention to finance, especially to financial change over time. In higher education, unfortunately, the attention has often been cursory and the product superficial, resulting in such proclamations as "Funding per student has declined by 6 percent in real dollars during the last five years," or "State support has not kept pace with inflation and enrollments," or "By 1990, instructional expenditures per full-time equivalent lower-division student will have lagged 20 percent behind increases in the Consumer Price Index," or "Our community college has lost one-third of its purchasing power since 1977."

Despite the diversity of approaches behind these and other assertions, most measures of financial adequacy could barely pass even elementary analytical tests. In fact, the higher education research community really has no general methodology for measuring financial adequacy over time, although there are several distinct approaches (see Gomberg and Altelsek, 1981; Minter, 1979; and Halstead, 1985). Even though this chapter does not present a comprehensive approach, it intends to identify some general guidelines for researchers that are useful, analytically appropriate, and relatively simple.

P. M. Callan (ed.). *Environmental Scanning for Strategic Leadership.*
New Directions for Institutional Research, no. 52. San Francisco: Jossey-Bass, Winter 1986.

Introduction to Fiscal Measurement in Higher Education

To compare funding changes over time, most studies use the measure of total education and general dollars per full-time equivalent student, deflated by some economic index (see Halstead, 1985). Although perhaps such a procedure is unavoidable at the highly aggregated level of state and national analysis, a competent review of institutional resources over time would never rely on any single measure. At the least, an institutional review would begin by separating cost changes into those necessary to maintain existing programs, those that take account of workload fluctuations, and those that result from policies to enhance the institution or to cut back its programs.

Putting these ideas another way, Robinson and others (1977) argue that such behavior is influenced by three types of forces:

- Environmental factors: conditions influencing cost behavior, which exist in the social, economic, political, cultural, and physical milieus in which the institution operates but over which the institution has no substantial control.
- Volume factors: the behavior of costs in reaction to changes in the volume of a defined range of activities or services for a given period of time.
- Decision factors: the specific attributes or elements of goals, objectives, programs, organizational structure, and operating policies, which can be directly and substantially affected by decisions of administrators.

Obviously, the practical problems of measuring these factors are forbidding, but I believe the categories do identify the most important differences in cost behavior that must be taken into account in a sound analysis of institutional finance. Furthermore, if simplified, these categories can be useful in measuring changes in resources within an institution. For example, this chapter will use the effects of inflation as a rough proxy for environmental factors, and enrollment change for volume factors, although research into a specific institution's finances should employ additional measures. Space limits here force us to ignore decision factors, although these are often the most important for the vitality or demise of an educational institution.

Measuring the Impact of Inflation on Higher Education

Inflation has different impacts among the activities in higher education. Educational expenditures are traditionally organized into programs (instruction, academic support, student services, institutional support, and so on) or into objects (salaries, fringe benefits, utilities, library acquisitions, supplies, electronic equipment, and so on). Research into inflation's impact on an institution is best begun by using the "object" categories, since programs can mix the cost components that contain the largest inflation differentials.

If the rate of price change in our economy were relatively uniform, then the impact of inflation on purchasing power for the goods and services purchased in higher education would be roughly equal. Unfortunately, the rate of price change is anything but uniform, even during times of low inflation, as shown in Figure 1.

This figure suggests that the *rate* of increase for some items purchased by institutions of higher education was roughly twice that of others during the past ten years. Thus, buying the "same" quantity of fringe benefits in 1984 would cost roughly six times more than in 1971, while the "cost" of professional salaries increased by "only" 250 percent over the same period.

Rather than using some overall inflation measure for all institutional expenditures, the analysis should use different inflation rates, chosen from appropriate indices among the budget's major components, and then

Figure 1. Trends in Higher Education Cost Components; 1971 = 100

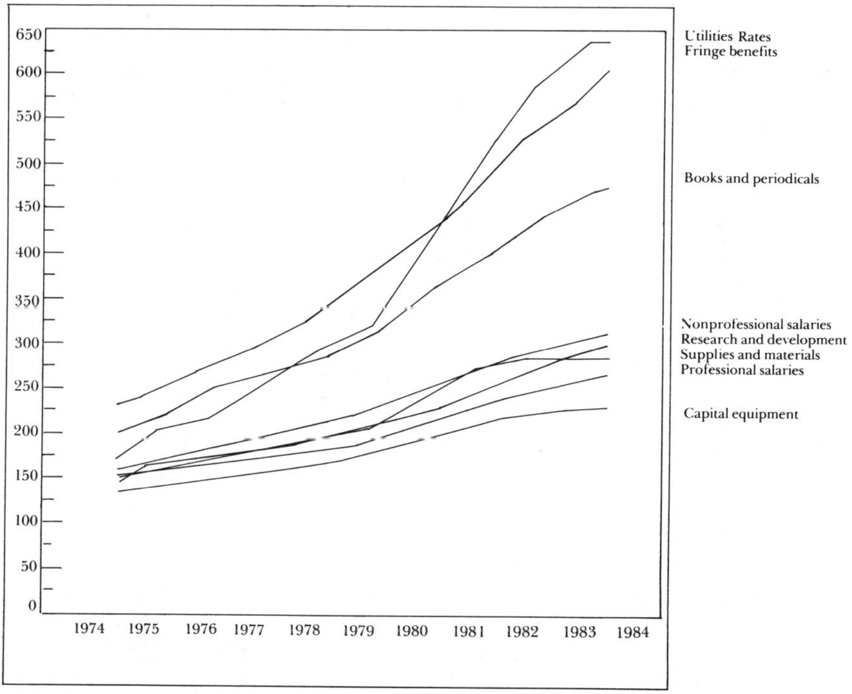

Source: Research Associates of Washington, 1985.

weight those rates by the proportion of total institutional expenditures represented by each component.

No single index is appropriate to measure inflation in every area. A price index is a statistical measure of the effects of price change *only* (not of changes in the quantity or quality of goods) for a fixed number of items. However, in an economy as complicated as ours, economists use numerous indices to measure inflation, and this practice challenges reliance on any single measure. During times of relatively low inflation, such as in the recent past, the differences between these measures are small. However, during times of rapid price increases (and such times constitute at least some portion of almost any time series), the divergence between indices can be troublesome.

As an example, Table 1 displays the annual percentage increases in the Consumer Price Index (CPI) and the Implicit Price Deflator for the Gross National Product (GNP), the two most widely recognized measures of inflation. As shown, the divergence between these two measures in 1979 (4.7 percent) was considerable, while divergences have been within 0.2 percent for the most recent years. All this suggests that no single index is appropriate in every instance, especially in a complex environment like higher education. The following paragraphs describe the four major indexes most useful in higher education and the ways they might be used by researchers.

The Consumer Price Index (CPI). The CPI measures the price change of a constant "market basket" of goods and services typically purchased by consumers. Extensive data on the CPI are available from the Department of Commerce, Bureau of Economic Analysis, Washington, D.C.

Advantages. The CPI is issued monthly and is reported by regions of the country. Although it is a measure of consumer prices, most of the expenditures in postsecondary education are for salaries, which are affected by changes in consumer prices. Therefore, it is a reasonable measure of the adequacy of at least one component of expenditures.

Table 1. Percentage Increases in the Consumer Price Index (CPI) and Gross National Product Deflator (GNP) (December to December)

Year	*CPI*	*GNP*
1976	+4.8%	+5.2%
1977	6.8%	5.8%
1978	9.0%	7.4%
1979	13.3%	8.6%
1980	11.5%	9.2%
1981	8.9%	9.6%
1982	3.9%	6.0%
1983	3.8%	3.8%
1984	4.0%	3.8%

Source: U.S. Council of Economic Advisers, 1985.

Disadvantages. The CPI is rigid in its fixed "market basket" and until recently has included a home-ownership component that overemphasizes changes in mortgage rates. Many economists agree that "the CPI is a seriously flawed index" (Gordon, 1981, p. 134).

The Personal Consumption Expenditures Index (PCE). The PCE index measures the prices of a changing "market basket" of goods and services, based on actual purchases, and has used a "rental equivalent" index for housing, rather than the costs of home ownership—a more realistic approach. The PCE is also available from the Department of Commerce, Bureau of Economic Analysis, Washington, D.C.

Advantages. The PCE is generally believed to better reflect the actual behavior of consumers than does the CPI, since it realistically assumes that people change their purchasing patterns when relative prices among goods change. The "rental equivalence" measure is preferable to the total cost of buying a house, since it is not so sensitive to swings in mortgage rates. The PCE is a reasonable measure of price changes facing employees in postsecondary institutions. Since most institutional expenditures compensate employees, this index is useful in determining if salaries are lagging behind price increases.

Disadvantages. The PCE is published quarterly and does not have a regional component. Therefore, price differences among regions of the nation, an important consideration in educational finance, are not adequately captured by the PCE.

The State and Local Goods and Services Deflator. This index is designed to measure price changes of the goods and services purchased by governments, rather than those purchased by consumers (the CPI or PCE) or in the United States economy as a whole (the GNP deflator). It includes expenditures by state governments, local governments, and educational institutions for equipment and all capital goods, salaries and benefits, and contract purchases. It excludes grants to individuals (transfer payments) and subventions from state to local governments. This index is available from the Department of Commerce.

Advantages. This index better measures the nonsalary increases in postsecondary education than do either the CPI or the PCE. Since consumers do not purchase most of the items used in educational institutions, this index better reflects the realities facing administrators. It also eliminates any bias that housing or rental equivalents might have on the index, an inappropriate item for measuring price changes in higher education.

Disadvantages. The index is heavily influenced by purchases in agencies and activities outside postsecondary education, most of which are quite distinct from purchases in educational institutions. Also, the index measures expenditures that result more from the amount of revenue governments have available than from the actual costs of goods and services.

The Higher Education Price Index (HEPI). This index measures average changes in the prices of goods and services purchased by colleges and universities through their current education and general funds. The quantities of these goods and services are kept constant, based on the 1971-1972 purchasing pattern. The weights assigned to the various elements represent their relative importance in the current-fund educational and general budget and are estimated national averages. Obviously, the index is dominated by the trend in faculty salaries and trends for other personnel hired by the institutions. The HEPI is available from Research Associates of Washington, 2605 Klingle Road N.W., Washington, D.C. 20008.

Advantages. This is the only index that measures the changes in goods and services purchased exclusively in higher education. In addition, data are available to track changes in professional salaries, nonprofessional salaries, fringe benefits, contracted services, supplies and materials, equipment, books and periodicals, and utilities. The HEPI is distinct from the Higher Education Research and Development Price Index, which measures changes faced by universities through current expenditures for sponsored research. It is important to separate this component of higher education, since, for instance, sponsored research requires nearly twice the relative number of contracted services, supplies, materials, and equipment as the current educational and general budgets of colleges. As shown in Figure 1, the differences in the rates of change among these components are sufficiently large to justify segregation of sponsored research in measuring inflation.

Disadvantages. This index measures a fixed mix of goods and services established many years ago. Because of changes in relative prices among goods and services, most institutions have changed the mix of purchases since then, thus making the index less than an accurate measure for the actual increases facing any single institution. Also, the method of financing higher education differs significantly from that in commercial enterprises, because public institutions generally spend the revenue available to them. Thus, changes in salaries and other expenditures are more often measures of the availability of funds than of need or of salary changes that might have occurred without the rigid staffing patterns predominant in higher education.

Which index should higher education researchers use? Any one of them may be used, so long as the measurement purpose is clear. For instance, if the purpose were to show how general price changes are covered by the expenditures of postsecondary institutions, then the Higher Education Price Index would be most appropriate. Sometimes one of the HEPI's components would be best for a specific investigation; but if the purpose were to measure the need for increased expenditures, in terms of how much should have been spent for salaries if they were to have kept up with inflation, then one of the consumer indexes (the CPI or the PCE) would be more appropriate. The State and Local Government Goods and Services Deflator would be best for measuring how higher education expenditures compare with overall increases in state and local expenditure patterns.

Measuring the Impact of Workload Changes

Using total educational and general dollars per full-time equivalent student to assess the adequacy of funding changes over time assumes that the cost of adding students is the same as the average cost of all students currently enrolled. This is incorrect, both conceptually and (in an increasing number of states) practically. It is surprising that this technique has any credibility left at all in institutional research.

Conceptually, the cost of educating additional students in one year is usually less than the average cost for all students. This is so because any producer of goods and services, whether public or private, incurs certain fixed costs, regardless of the operation's size. Buildings must be maintained, utility bills must be paid, and management must function to some degree. The total cost of an educational institution is the sum of these fixed costs, plus variable costs (those directly related to the size of the student body). The average cost of education is the total cost of all campus activities related directly or indirectly to instruction, divided by the number of students. The marginal cost, or incremental cost, represents the dollars necessary to instruct additional students in existing programs. For most time-series analysis, the marginal cost rate is preferable.

Average cost is high initially, since an institution must staff up to some critical mass of program array and student services before opening its doors. Then, the cost of adding students is nominal, because they fill existing programs and courses. These additional students also place minimal demands on librarians, counselors, and other support staff. As the college grows, however, the courses are filled, and entirely new offerings and services should be established. This means high costs for any students added just above a certain enrollment level. After new programs and services are in place, the marginal costs are reduced until the need to expand again becomes compelling. Thus, costs rise quickly, reach a plateau, and rise quickly again, as shown in Figure 2.

What does this well-aspected theory imply for measuring the cost of additional students over time? Clearly, the use of average cost is justifiable, if ever, only during periods of sustained and large-scale growth. If an institution is growing slowly—say, 20 percent over a decade—the proper measure to be applied to the additional students is not the average cost, but the marginal cost or some proxy for it. Usually marginal cost is less than average cost—but how much less?

Figure 2. The Cost Increase for an Institution with Enrollment Growth

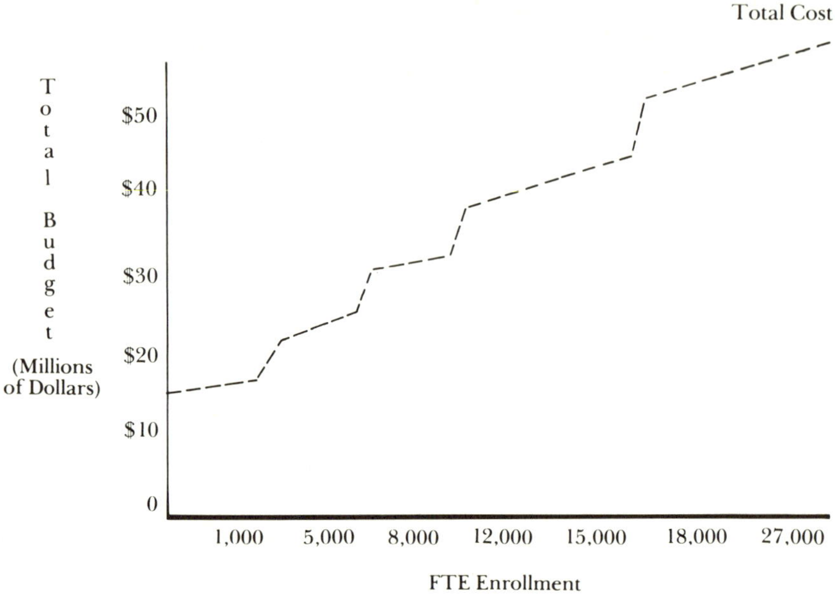

To answer this, we should examine the practical world of appropriations and the ways that states fund enrollment changes in their formulas (see Allen and Topping, 1979; Pickens, 1980, pp. 15-22). Earlier, most states did reimburse institutions at the average cost, since this was the simplest approach, but most are changing. A number of states have established different measures of workload for budget categories outside the instructional program; student services, research, public service, administration, and plant maintenance are the ones most often removed from enrollment as a funding measure. Alternately, some states have established a portion of costs that are considered fixed and do not change with enrollment. Still others have assigned an arbitrary percentage of the average cost, usually between one-half and two-thirds, as a proxy for calculating the cost impact of enrollment increases or declines.

A review of enrollment funding studies suggests that over some range (say, enrollment increases of less than 20 percent), the cost of adding additional students should be assumed to have been covered if a mature institution received two-thirds of its average expenditure per full-time equivalent for the additional students (see, for example, Steen, 1979, pp. 28-29; Ohio Board of Regents, 1979, p. 132; California Community Colleges, 1980, pp. 19-20). Likewise, the actual savings that result from enrollment declines of less than 20 percent in a large college over several years, should be assumed for analytical purposes to be roughly two-thirds the average cost.

Identifying the Proper Base Year

After choosing an appropriate deflator and accurately accounting for the fiscal implications of enrollment changes, the most important step in measuring resources over time is selecting an appropriate initial or base year.

Any reputable text in statistics warns that the length of a time series can be manipulated to prove a conclusion. In financial analysis, the opportunities for such manipulation abound and are often evident, although probably as much by inadvertence as by mischievous design. Let me offer two examples from our work in California.

The community colleges in California have complained bitterly about the erosion of their resources since Proposition 13. Quite reasonably (on the surface of it), their analysis has used the year before that proposition, 1977, as the point of departure in measuring their fiscal losses per full-time equivalent student. However, as Figure 3 shows, a longer time series can yield a number of different conclusions, primarily because revenues per student were at an all-time high in 1977–1978. Further, one could argue that the colleges have been well-financed since 1982–1983—a period they portray as a "dark age" in funding—because their inflation-adjusted per-student revenues have increased by 9.7 percent. Much of this increase, of course, is the formulated result of massive enrollment declines statewide, which, according to statute, do not result in the colleges' losing the average cost per student. Therefore, a smaller amount of total revenues is spread over a much smaller number of students, thus rapidly increasing the revenues per student.

A second example comes from the California Postsecondary Education Commission's (1981) review of a request from the California State University for a large salary increase in 1981–1982. The request was based on the assertion that the purchasing power of faculty salaries had declined since 1968 by 26.7 percent. Our review indicated that while the mathematics of their calculated lag were correct, such a large erosion could be obtained only by combining one specific year as base (1968–1969) with the index (CPI) that had increased the most since that year. Any other combinations resulted in less of a lag, and some even showed a gain in purchasing power (pp. 8–9).

The point is that the initial year in any time series is crucial; clearly, results using several base years should be examined. The date finally selected should be early enough to encompass one complete cycle or show a steady progression. In addition, data can be analyzed by using several simple statistical tests to identify bimodal distributions, closely related clusters, or statistically significant changes between certain years.

Whatever the result, it is important to remember that any base year highlights certain conclusions or obscures others. The burden of proof should fall squarely on the researcher to demonstrate that this has not occurred with deceitful intentions.

Figure 3. Revenues per Full-Time Equivalent Student in the California Community Colleges (in Constant Dollars)

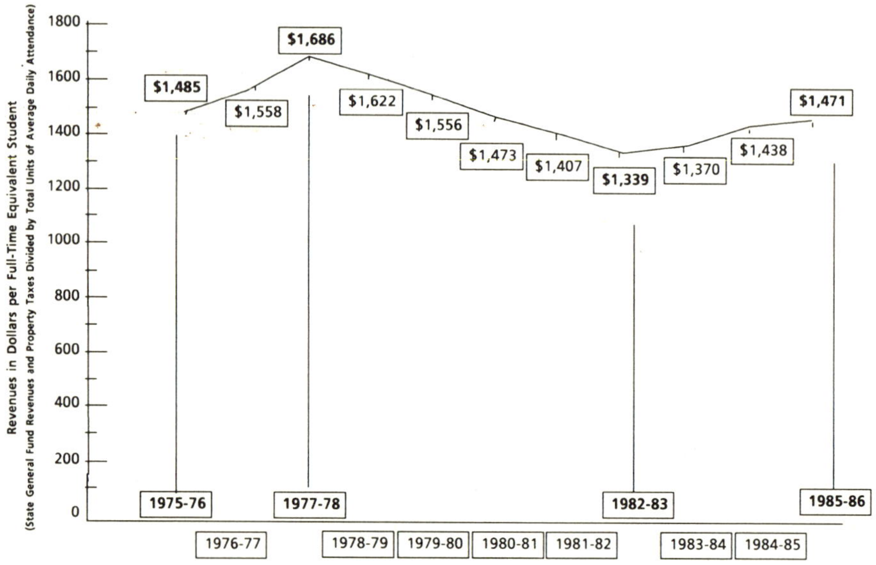

Conclusion

To be credible, institutional research should include fiscal planning and some estimates of the resources required for various scenarios. As background for these exercises, the research should present measurements of the adequacy of past resources. The researcher should at least determine how best to measure the effects of inflation on institutional resources over time, how to estimate the resource implications of enrollment changes and other workload adjustments, and how to identify the cost of policy changes in the quality or extent of educational services.

The main point of this chapter is to suggest that determining the level of "real" resources over time is a difficult business and should not be approached casually. At a minimum, a sound analysis should adopt the following protocols:

1. Several measures of inflation should be used and the purpose of each clearly identified. For instance, one measure might determine price increases in fixed costs, and another might measure the effect of inflation on the purchasing power of employee salaries.
2. Over some range (certainly up to 20 percent), the analysis should assume that full funding of enrollment changes did occur if two-

thirds of the average expenditure per full-time equivalent student was provided.

3. The analysis should demonstrate that the initial or base year in the time series was not chosen to prove a specific conclusion.

References

Allen, R. H., and Topping, J. R. (eds.). *Cost Information and Formula Funding: New Approaches.* Boulder, Colo.: National Center for Higher Education Management Systems, 1979.

California Community Colleges. *Incremental Cost Study.* Sacramento: The Chancellor's Office, January 1980.

California Postsecondary Education Commission. *Final Annual Report on Faculty Salaries in California Public Higher Education, 1981-82.* Sacramento: California Postsecondary Education Commission, 1981.

Gomberg, I. L., and Atelsek, F. J. *Trends in Financial Indicators of Colleges and Universities.* Washington, D.C.: American Council on Education, 1981.

Gordon, R. "The Consumer Price Index: Measuring Inflation and Causing It." *The Public Interest,* 1981, *63,* 112-134.

Halstead, D. K. *How States Compare in Financial Support of Higher Education, 1984-85.* Washington, D.C.: National Institute of Education, 1985.

Minter, W. J. "Current Economic Trends in American Higher Education." *Change Magazine,* 1979, *11* (1), 19-25.

Ohio Board of Regents. *A Strategic Approach to the Maintenance of Institutional Financial Stability and Flexibility in the Face of Enrollment Instability or Decline.* Washington, D.C.: Academy for Educational Development, 1979.

Pickens, W. H. *Statewide Formulas to Support Higher Education.* Washington, D.C.: National Conference of State Legislatures, 1980.

Research Associates of Washington. *Higher Education Price Index, Update for 1984.* Washington, D.C.: Research Associates of Washington, 1985.

Robinson, D. D., Ray, H. W., and Turk, F. J. "Cost Behavior Analysis for Planning in Higher Education." *Professional File of the National Association of College and University Business Officers,* 1977, *9* (5), 1-51.

Steen, R. W. *The Texas Formula System.* Austin: The State of Texas, 1979.

U.S. Council of Economic Advisers. *Economic Indicators.* Washington, D.C.: U.S. Government Printing Office, March 1985.

William H. Pickens assumed the executive directorship of the California Postsecondary Education Commission in August 1986, where formerly he was director of fiscal analysis with responsibilities for following all fiscal legislation affecting postsecondary institutions in California.

College and university information is poorly developed for the purpose of making strategic choices and management guidance. A strategic triangle, with critical success factors at each vertex, can help model appropriate information.

Information System Requirements for Strategic Choices

Robert G. Cope

It has been observed that college and university planning has evolved through four stages: budget planning, goal and objective setting, forecasting, and strategic planning (Heydinger, 1983). The concept of strategic planning places new demands on institutional researchers. The technically oriented information requirements of the 1970s will need to be augmented with managerially oriented systems. Precisely what this will mean for higher education is still unclear; however, it is clear that the new information will cost less, will be simplified, and will be more directly related to the long-term success of the institution (Rockart, 1982).

Most institutional information systems, whether computerized or not, were originally designed for and provide internal and historical information. Strategic choices require more information, largely in the form of intelligence (unstructured, subjective, quickly assembled, but credible and reliable) about future and future-oriented external conditions (Cope, 1985; Morrison and others, 1985).

This chapter describes a strategic triangle (Ohmae, 1983) for systematic information gathering in order to support two types of decisions: those related to strategic choices and to guidance and control. It also

P. M. Callan (ed.). *Environmental Scanning for Strategic Leadership.*
New Directions for Institutional Research, no. 52. San Francisco: Jossey-Bass, Winter 1986.

describes critical success factors that help to determine the specific information required for strategic choices and central decisions within the triangle construct (Sullivan, 1985).

The Strategic Triangle

The utility of the triangle concept lies in its simplicity. Reduced to its essentials, effective strategy deals with the interplay of three entities: the institution; its competitors; and various stakeholders, including students, agencies of government, foundations, alumni, communities, and so on. Any entity affected by the institution becomes a stakeholder for the purpose of strategy formulation (Mitroff, 1983).

Stakeholder information must include trend analyses on application rates, admitted students, indices of student quality, retention to graduation ratios, changing characteristics over time, and so on. Additional stakeholder information, depending on the institution, would include anticipated initiatives in government-sponsored research, changing initiatives of foundations, the attitudes of alumni, and so on. Competitor information would describe competing institutions in terms of such things as faculty salaries and benefits, levels of student financial aid offered, new program ventures, accreditation reviews, and tuition levels. Institutional information would characterize the institution itself on indices of program quality, market viability, faculty turnover, and costs.

Critical Success Factors

Critical success factors are those few key variables about which reliable data are absolutely necessary to make wise strategic choices and to assess progress toward goals. Some critical success factors are universally important (student numbers and quality, for example). Others, however, may depend on strategic choices already made. When Rensselaer Polytechnic Institute, for example, decided to broaden its base of recruitment,

Figure 1. The Strategic Triangle

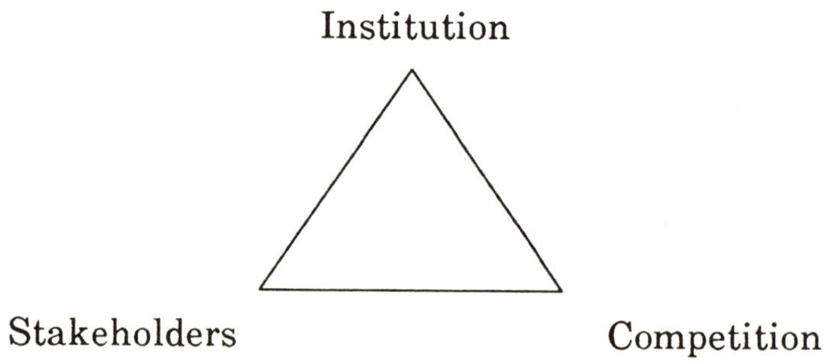

declining numbers of students from its traditional service area were a critical consideration. When a private liberal arts college in a midwestern city decided to increase its tuition, moving it from the bottom third into the top third for costs among institutions in its zone of competition, the low tuitions charged among competing institutions were a critical factor. When the University of Michigan decided to shift, over five years, millions of dollars out of some colleges and into others, the changing demand ratios were critical to that decision.

As the triangle concept implies, a successful strategy must consider critical success factors of all three types of factors. A strategic decision changes the institution, its stakeholders, and its competition. Over ten years ago, Rensselaer Polytechnic Institute announced that it would become the most computerized American university, initiated recruiting and job-placement activities in selected locations in other parts of the country, and developed new contractual relationships with high-technology businesses. In so doing, it changed the institution, it developed new communities of stakeholders, and it further differentiated itself from competing institutions. These were strategic changes based on strategic choices. Each institution must develop its own critical success factors, depending on its unique situation and leading to a distinctive strategy.

Information Follows Purposes

The information demands placed on the institutional researcher are changing. Strategic planning (the process), the choices made, and resulting controls require far less information than is commonly available, and the information is needed selectively, infrequently, on an aggregated basis, and with low accuracy. Figure 2 contrasts characteristics of useful information across three purposes.

For the purpose of understanding and eventually designing distinctive institution-based and academic unit–based information requirements, some additional distinctions are useful. A *datum* is understood to mean a single element or a fact. Information is an aggregate of data so utilized as to become knowledge. Data, as such, have no intrinsic significance until they become information, and information itself is meaningless until related to some purpose. The information that is the subject of this chapter serves three kinds of institutional purposes: those of operations, control, and strategic planning. The discussion's emphasis, however, is on strategic and controlling purposes, since that is where the deficiencies are currently greatest.

Information for the purposes of guidance and control involves year-to-year tactical decisions about the deployment of resources and their effective and efficient application. Information for strategic purposes aids in the delineation of alternative courses of direction that have time horizons of from three to ten years away. Operational information is for mainte-

Figure 2. Characteristics of Information and Institutional Purpose

Characteristic	Purpose: Strategic Planning	Tactical Planning/ Management Control and Guidance	Operational Control
Time horizon	present and future	←→	past and present
Source of information	external	←→	internal
Type of information	qualitative	←→	quantitative
Level of detail	aggregate	←→	detailed
Accuracy	low	←→	high
Range of variables	wide	←→	narrow
Frequency of use	infrequent	←→	frequent
Currency of information	low	←→	high

Source: Arns and Curran, 1982.

nance. Information for control is for managing and guiding the institution. Information for strategic purposes is for adjusting to developing new situations. Adjusting to new situations requires the selective gathering of data and converting it to information, then to knowledge, and ultimately to sound strategic choices.

The deficiencies are now greatest at the strategic level, where planning capabilities are currently the least developed, as a result of the four-stage process of development noted earlier (budget planning, goal and objectives setting, forecasting, and strategic planning). As each form of planning has arisen, appropriate supporting information systems have also been developed.

Operational information is maintained on a day-to-day basis in order to record and ensure performance. It is a highly accurate and detailed record of the past and the present about students, expenditures, facilities, and so on, yet it is of little value in strategic planning. It is gathered as unfocused by-products of operating system requirements. Reports from the operating system are essentially spinoffs from a system designed to perform routine, bottom-up paperwork processing. The transition from operational information to strategic planning information is not a natural one. The need for operational information is legitimate, and institutional researchers will continue to serve this function. However, the researcher must find the time and resources to introduce external, qualitative, future-oriented information into the institutional decision process.

Strategic Choice

Strategic choice involves a major decision altering the relationship of the institution to its environment. Too often, any important decision is considered strategic. The key word is *environment.* A strategic decision alters the institution's resource-acquisition or resource-depletion relationship with the environment. A decision to establish a new off-campus center alters the institution's relationship with its environment. The choice of the center's director is only a means to implement the strategic choice. Deciding to recruit more students from selected communities is strategic. Offering them more choices of work-study programs is operational. A university's decision to give greater emphasis to community relations is strategic. Deciding on a number of ways to do this is implementation. One institution's decision to become known as the "most computerized institution" is strategic. Another institution's decision to install a computer system of similar capacity might be operational if, for example, its purpose were the establishment of a detailed accountability system where none existed, in response to federal or state government desires for greater accountability.

Strategy determines the nature and the direction of the institution. Strategic choices relate to scope of services, choice of those served, growth considerations, and the nature of relationships with other organizations. Strategic choices deal with "what" rather than "how." Strategy determines appropriate goals and objectives, which, however defined, follow from strategy and determine critical success factors. These factors are the key variables used for guiding and controlling the institution's movements in accord with agreed-upon strategies. Thus, they bear on the middle set of information identified in Figure 2.

Consistent with the idea that there are two levels of strategy in every moderately complex institution, each strategic academic or strategic business unit will have different critical success factors. Thus, information needs are tailored by level, by strategic choices, by managerial preferences, and by time.

Computers or Intelligence

Much strategic information is in the form of unstructured intelligence. Intelligence is future-oriented, quickly assembled, subjective, and often delivered by word of mouth from creditable sources. The strongest advocates of strategic planning may indeed conclude that all computer-based reports will be useless for strategy. Figure 3 illustrates the relationship between the types of decisions and decision-supporting information systems suggested here.

Figure 3. Examples of Types of Decisions and Decision-Supporting Information Systems

	Operations	Management	Strategic
Structured	Billing students Registrar's records	Admission of students Class registration	Mix of students
Semistructured	Class scheduling Inventory control	Cost analysis Fund management	Location of functions
	Computer Useful		
Unstructured	Installation of PERT	New equipment or marketing effort	New degree programs

As decisions become less structured, less routine, and less frequent and move away from operating tasks, the need increases for environmental scanning, intelligence, and the application of wisdom in decision making.

In summary, data and information systems usually reflect transactions made in functional units (admissions, accounts payable, and so on) and provide information from the bottom up. By beginning with strategies and ideas about indicators of successful movement (the critical success factors), one reverses the process by which institutions develop information systems.

The job of supplementing existing data and information systems is not so imposing as it may seem at first, because there are only limited key variables to capture, and some are temporal. The list of factors will differ from institution to institution, from strategic academic unit to unit, and from one set of personal preferences to another set of personal preferences.

Although they may not be obvious, there are at least three benefits to developing sets of information by following the strategic triangle and its related critical success factors.

1. Managers, chairpersons, presidents, deans, and so on gain clarity about factors requiring attention. The process of determining strategy and critical success factors ensures that significant factors receive scrutiny.
2. Identifying critical success factors allows for a limited definition of the amounts and kinds of information that must be collected.
3. Acknowledging the temporal nature of the information requirements renders the information system dynamic, with new formats of reports accompanying new ways of thinking about strategic choices.

The shift to strategic information will not replace the traditional functions of the institutional research office, but its inclusion in the functions of the office will be of growing importance to the institution.

References

Arns, R. G., and Curran, F. A. "Information System Requirements for Strategic Planning and Implementation." Paper presented at the CAUSE National Conference, Hilton Head Island, South Carolina, December 1982.

Cope, R. G. "A Contextual Model to Encompass the Strategic Planning Concept: Introducing a Newer Paradigm." *Planning for Higher Education,* 1985, *13* (3), 13-20.

Heydinger, R. B. "Using External Information in Planning: Some Tools for Expanding Our Vision and Enhancing Our Strategic Thinking." Paper presented at the Conference on Academic Renewal, Center for the Study of Higher Education, University of Michigan, Ann Arbor, June 1983.

Mitroff, I. I. *Stakeholders of the Organizational Mind.* San Francisco: Jossey-Bass, 1983.

Morrison, J. L., Renfro, W. L., and Boucher, W. I. *Futures Research and the Strategic Planning Process.* Washington, D.C.: Association for the Study of Higher Education, 1984.

Ohmae, K. "The 'Strategic Triangle' and Business Unit Strategy." *The McKinsey Quarterly,* Winter 1983, 9-24.

Rockart, J. F. "The Changing Role of the Information Systems Executive: A Critical Success Factors Perspective." *Sloan Management Review,* 1982, *24* (1), 3-13.

Sullivan, C. H. "Systems Planning in the Information Age." *Sloan Management Review,* 1985, *26* (2), 3-12.

Robert G. Cope is associate professor of policy, governance, and administration at the University of Washington in Seattle.

Environmental scanning efforts at three different levels of service area—community, regional, statewide—illustrate its utility for institutional and agency planning.

Examples of Strategic Planning at Several Levels

Keith G. Pailthorp

This chapter describes long-range planning in the San Francisco Community College District, an urban two-year college district; the University of Nevada, Reno, a public state university; and the California Postsecondary Education Commission, a statewide coordinating board working with a complex set of public and private institutions. These three case studies illustrate the use of demographic and economic information in constructing a basis for policy determination. They describe the mechanisms established for ongoing environmental monitoring and the strategic decisions that have resulted from this monitoring. Beyond this, they highlight the strengths and weaknesses of the scanning and planning process pursued in each instance, in search of "dos" and "don'ts" for the reader.

The San Francisco Community College District

The San Francisco Community College District was established in 1970. It consists of two divisions—the City College of San Francisco, estab-

The author is indebted to Tyra Duncan-Hall, executive assistant to the chancellor, San Francisco Community College District, and to Richard O. Davies, vice-president for academic affairs, University of Nevada, Reno, for making available the considerable documentation of their institution's exemplary planning efforts.

P. M. Callan (ed.). *Environmental Scanning for Strategic Leadership.*
New Directions for Institutional Research, no. 52. San Francisco: Jossey-Bass, Winter 1986.

lished in 1935, and the Community College Centers (formerly the Adult Education/Adult Occupational Education Division), dating from 1856. In 1983, City College enrolled over 29,000 day and evening students, while the eight Community College Centers enrolled some 40,000 students in noncredit day and evening classes offered in over 250 district-owned, rented, or donated facilities. Half of the Centers' workload is in classes in English as a Second Language (ESL).

In 1982, a new chancellor assumed responsibility for the district. That fall he initiated two major projects: a comprehensive review of the district's instructional programs, and the development of a long-range educational master plan for the district. One can second-guess the decision to conduct these two efforts in parallel, since the existence of the program review might have heightened anxieties over the long-range planning effort. However, there is no indication of adverse interaction having occurred.

The team that the chancellor assembled to develop the educational master plan and produce a mechanism for ongoing continuous planning—the District Planning Council—consisted of two board members, six faculty members, twelve administrators, and three classified staff members. They, in turn, empaneled six districtwide task forces—on instructional services, facilities, fiscal support, student support services, personnel, and public information. The eighteen members of each of these task forces included faculty, administrators, classified staff, and community and business representatives. Institutional research staff of the district assisted the council and the task forces; but, clearly, master planning was not to be an inside job.

The institutional research staff was fortunate that the district's master planning effort followed closely on the heels of the San Francisco Chamber of Commerce's completion of a strategic plan for the entire community. Not only were district staff members able to draw on the broader planning done in developing that document; they also had access to a network of agencies and organizations that had been involved in the prior effort and that proved indispensable in their ongoing planning.

The other asset that the staff and the District Planning Council started with was the new chancellor's commitment to the concept of continuous planning and monitoring of the district's external environment and his continuing involvement in many San Francisco Bay Area groups representing the leaders of business, industry, government, and education, which complemented the information network of the staff.

With the staff's help, the District Planning Council produced a 160-page plan that set the context for planning by assessing the district's external and internal environments. The external factors included population growth, race and ethnicity, immigrants and refugees, the aging of the population, changes in marital status, the handicapped, educational attainment (particularly for the various ethnic groups), changes in elementary and secondary school enrollment patterns, projections of high school graduates, language diversity, income and economic status, the cost of living, employment trends, labor force skills, "collar" classification, and major industries (present and future). Nonlocal external factors included California Community College funding mechanisms, finance legislation, and governance.

Internal factors included enrollment trends and projections; the ethnicity, citizenship, sex, age, educational attainment, educational objectives, course loads, household occupations and incomes, and financial aid profiles of students; faculty and staff profiles in terms of sex, age, ethnicity, years of service, and academic qualifications; degrees and certificates awarded; and shifts in student interests.

This broad and thorough environmental snapshot became the heart of the planning document. Without collecting any new data, it drew together and synthesized the perspectives of public and private agencies far beyond the district, to form a picture of the demographic and economic outlook for San Francisco County. In so doing, it placed City College and the Community College Centers in a context that prevented the natural reversion to institutional isolation. As an example of this context, in many ways San Francisco County is more like urban centers in the East than it is like other California cities. Its population is not projected to grow; it cannot, because of space limitations. In fact, the county's population has actually declined since 1960. Its population is also old by California standards (with a 1980 median age of 33.9 years) and aging (with a year-2000 median age expected to be 42.7 years), largely because families cannot afford to live in the city. San Francisco has a larger proportion of single households than any other city in the nation. At the same time, the Bay Area, and San Francisco in particular, is the nation's second major port of entry (behind Los Angeles) for Asian immigrants and refugees. These and other unique features of the district made for an intriguing planning problem.

The second part of the planning document described the planning process, including extensive efforts to ensure broad involvement and to build consensus; the goals established by the six task forces; a mechanism for integrating these goals and strategies with program review, accreditation, and budgeting; and the obligatory mission statement. Interestingly, this mission statement gave no hint of the thorough, systematic planning effort that preceded it. It was labeled "a broad statement of an institution's fundamental purposes" and "the social and intellectual aspirations of an institution . . . a philosophical, value-oriented declaration that describes the continuing responsibilities of the institution and suggests their relative importance." With a few name changes, it could serve as a statement of purpose for almost any urban community college district in the country.

A companion document set out an ambitious agenda of ongoing planning. It detailed the strategies arrived at by the six task forces to achieve the goals they had identified in the master plan. It also included the Planning Council's assessment of each strategy as either presently implementable, not currently implementable, or in need of further study.

A third document listed resources and contact people from state agencies, national organizations, libraries, local agencies, and private organizations involved in futures research and included an annotated bibliography of publications from these sources.

The master planning effort of the district was instructive, given its broad range of participants, the thoroughness of its environmental assessment, its reliance on available information, and the quality of its documentation. It is hard to imagine that anyone even tangentially involved in the effort could fail to have his or her perspective on the institution broadened.

The University of Nevada, Reno

Established in 1874 as Nevada's land-grant college, the University of Nevada, Reno (UNR) is the only four-year public institution in the northern half of the nation's most rapidly growing state. Nevada is one of only seven states projected for postsecondary enrollment increases in the 1990s by the Carnegie Commission on Higher Education. In the past quarter-century, UNR has grown from a small and limited institution into a middle-sized, multipurpose university, awarding some twenty different doctoral degrees. In the 1970s, UNR's headcount enrollment grew some 30 percent, but this growth was not reflected in full-time equivalent enrollments until the early 1980s. Although in an urban setting, UNR serves a vast area of northern Nevada, and its division of continuing education has grown in size and importance in recent years.

In 1980, the university developed its first ten-year academic master plan. This plan represented the first step in several years of planning activity that included the formal constitution of a university planning and budget team, a seventeen-member group broadly representative of the campus community. This team prepared a set of internal and external planning assumptions for the period from 1984 to 1990 and developed a university mission and goal statement, approved in February 1984, that is notable for distinguishing the university's mission from its goals. The mission statement is uncommonly brief and clear. It uses the term *selected* with respect to programs and activities, thus at least implying limits to the university's scope.

The master plan was clearly labeled as "an initial base from which systematic review and planning will occur," with a new long-range planning committee established to review the plan periodically and monitor its implementation. Development of the base entailed a thorough look at the university's environmental context (both state and national)—past, present, and possible future. Starting from the university's land-grant heritage and legacy, through the years of postwar enrollment growth to the lean fiscal years that immediately preceded the plan, it demonstrates the continuous interdependence of state and institution.

The shifting pattern of student characteristics—more upper-division students, in response to community college development; lower student credit loads, as a concomitant of commuting urban students; more older students, reflecting the demographics and the societal need for more recertification and in-service programs—supports the university's outlook of increased responsiveness to societal needs in terms of specialized research, specialized programs, continuing education, and public service consulting (as in the case of the more than sixty UNR faculty members who consulted with officials in the state's executive branch on various aspects of the proposed MX missile site).

Environmental considerations seem to play less of a role in current institutional decision making as one moves from independent to publicly supported institutions, from two-year to four-year institutions, and from developing to mature institutions. Thus, this public, doctoral-level institution is exemplary in its awareness of its environment and its place within that environment.

In February 1983, UNR's vice-president for academic affairs completed a comprehensive review of all the university's academic, service, and support programs—from the library all the way through intercollegiate athletics and up to the office of the academic vice-president—prudently stopping just short of the office of the president. This program review was the other shoe of a matched pair. The master plan had projected smooth if modest enrollment growth throughout the 1980s, but it had recognized the limits on resources for this growth. The comprehensive review reflected university officials' realization that "a decision to do one thing is a decision not to do another," as well as a refreshing conviction that one can and must make decisions circumscribed by fixed resources. The trade-off entailed the consolidation or phase-out of a number of programs in exchange for the development, as national "centers of excellence," of a dozen other programs, including infrastructure engineering, Basque studies, and water resource management. These twelve programs were coldly given priority for scarce resources and boldly expected to achieve national prominence among their peer programs. This strategic decision was not one calculated to win friends among the unchosen multitude.

Taken as a whole, the several years of planning at UNR appear to have placed the institution in a better posture with respect to its external environment, if not to its internal constituents. The internal mechanisms that the planning exercise set in place seem likely to outlive the inevitable controversy attending significant institutional change, and the strength of the UNR planning effort lies in its awareness of mission as derived from Nevada's people and environment.

The California Postsecondary Education Commission

While other states will have higher percentage rates of population growth over the remainder of the century, no other state will add as many people as California will—about eight million between 1980 and 2000. More important than the magnitude of this growth are the several changes that will occur in the age and ethnic composition and geographical distribution of California's population.

California is the archetypal baby-boom state, and the aging of California's baby boomers will wreak havoc with public services over the next several decades. In 1995, the number of Californians aged fifteen through twenty-nine will be 7 percent lower than in 1980. At the same time, the number of thirty- through forty-four-year-olds will have grown more than 50 percent.

Also in 1995, California's school-age population, from age five through seventeen, will become less than 50 percent non-Hispanic white. Around the year 2010, its total population will achieve this composition. Currently, one in eight California public school youths is identified as "limited English-proficient," and the number has grown some 250 percent in the past decade. The resultant disparities in high school completion and college preparation are important, not just for postsecondary planners but also for public policy makers and private industry across the board.

Because of the sheer number of colleges and universities in California—8 general campuses of the University of California, 19 campuses of the California State University, 106 California Community Colleges, and some 80 regionally accredited independent institutions—the geographical distribution of higher education services leaves few major gaps. However, the enrollment outlook for some institutions will be profoundly affected by the redistribution of population and economic activity from affected urban counties to neighboring suburban counties. While the population of the state as a whole will grow by about one-third in the last two decades of the twentieth century, Los Angeles County and the San Francisco Bay Area will grow at less than half that rate, and Riverside and San Bernardino Counties will nearly double in size.

The combination of the age shift, racial minority growth (particularly among the language-disadvantaged), and regional redistribution of population will inflict a "triple whammy" on higher education. The aging of California's population will alter the demand for particular educational programs and levels of instruction and thus will shift demand among types of institutions. The ethnic and racial shifts could affect overall levels of enrollment, but the impact will differ by type and location of institution. The regional redistribution of population means that some institutions will find themselves bursting at the seams, while neighboring peer institutions are shrinking.

In recognition of the complexity of the planning context for postsecondary education, the California Postsecondary Education Commission set out in 1983 to analyze demographic and economic trends and to establish a basis for reassessments of public policies for postsecondary education, including those enshrined in 1960 master plan for higher education, which for twenty-five years had served as the blueprint for growth and development of the largest system of postsecondary education in the world. The commission established two technical advisory committees, one on demographics and the other on economics, with representation from the systemwide offices of the Community Colleges, the State University, and the University of California; the State Department of Education; the independent colleges; private vocational schools; the legislative analyst; and the State Department of Finance, California's designated state census-data center. These technical advisory committees were augmented by interested parties from individual campuses. This process uncovered demographic and economic planning resources in county councils of government, in diverse departments of universities (ranging from urban planning to public health), in community college planning offices, and among private entrepreneurs. The linkage to data from the public schools and from the State Department of Education proved crucial to the study of higher education's enrollment outlook, and work continues to improve this exchange of information.

With the considerable assistance of its two advisory groups, the commission developed four background papers—one reviewing the nature and scope of master planning for California higher education since World War II, a second exploring social and economic trends and reviewing the speculations of the more plausible of the futurists, a third dealing with California's population and enrollment trends, and a fourth projecting California's probable economic growth and the prospects for financial support of postsecondary education.

In 1983, data from the 1980 Census were just becoming available. These data, in conjunction both with the comprehensive enrollment information already collected by the commission and the official population projections from the Department of Finance, provided the centerpiece of the demographic study. The first two of these data sources were used to determine participation rates by institution and course load for lower-division, upper-division, and graduate students by age, ethnicity, and county of origin. Using an in-house computer simulation model, commission staff supplemented the population projections from the Department of Finance with estimates of future ethnicity for each county. These projections, together with the specific participation rates, yielded estimates of future enrollment potential for each type of institution. More important than any single estimate, however, was the ability of the model to simulate the effect of any conceivable shifts in population and participation on statewide and institution-specific enrollment potential, as well as on the network of interested individuals and agencies established in the process of developing these four background papers.

In 1984, the state legislature established a citizen's commission to reassess the 1960 master plan for higher education in California, in light of the changed conditions of the state and its institutions. By the time of the first meeting of this citizens' group, the four background papers had been completed and were used as references by the citizens' commission in the preparation of a new master plan, scheduled for completion early in 1987. Meanwhile, California Postsecondary Education Commission staff are making the information from the prospectus project available to institutional researchers and planners at segmental and local institutional levels.

Summary

These three examples were chosen primarily because of their extensive recourse to the broader environment, and in this they are exemplary, but they instruct as much by their shortcomings as by their successes. Not surprisingly, these shortcomings have occurred in follow-through and ongoing institutionalization of the planning processes once the initial concerted planning efforts have been completed. The acid test for the San Francisco Community College District's strong beginning of master planning will be the implementation of its planned strategies and further articulation of its ongoing planning process. The operational test of recent planning at the University of Nevada, Reno, will be its ability to sustain over time its high level of institutional commitment to the state. The ultimate tests of the California Postsecondary Education Commission's prospectus project will be the extent to which the intersegmental and interagency networks developed for the project endure and expand and the degree to which emerging issues continue to be informed by the information base the project has established.

What these three examples illustrate is the need for institutions of higher education, and for the higher education enterprise at large, to look beyond next year's budget and beyond the limits of the enterprise and see ahead the changes in the environment. What these examples suggest is the need for planning at institutional and statewide levels, so that institutions will complement and reinforce one another across organizational boundaries. What these three examples confirm is that effective planning is not a one-shot proposition, but an ongoing process.

Keith G. Pailthorp is assistant director for planning and a postsecondary education administrator at the California Postsecondary Education Commission, where he has directed the commission's long-range planning project, "A Prospectus for California Postsecondary Education, 1985–2000."

This chapter offers information on materials regarding environmental scanning, as well as indicators to scan.

Sources of Assistance

Martin M. Ahumada, JB Lon Hefferlin

This concluding section offers information about materials on environmental scanning and then suggestions about sources of data for scanning, organized into the six facets of the environment described by Richard Jonsen in his opening chapter: demographic, economic, political, organizational, technological, and social-cultural.

Information on Scanning

Almost all recent books on management and planning refer at least implicitly to environmental scanning, and those on strategic planning refer to it explicitly, since such scanning is a major element of this approach to planning. For example, "An organization must be able to identify economic, strategic, and behavioral considerations that provide early warning that change may be needed," says Lorange (1985, p. 454), in urging managers to make "certain types of information gathering routine" by "creating more 'mechanistic' data inputs to the strategic decision-making process."

For other writers on the topic, from the perspective of general management, see Aguilar, 1967; Camillus, 1981; Drucker, 1980; Hegarty, 1981; Heydinger, 1983; Kast, 1980; Nanus, 1982; Renfro, 1984; and Vanderwicken, 1982.

Among scholars of higher education, the best known advocate of environmental scanning is James L. Morrison, professor of education at

P. M. Callan (ed.). *Environmental Scanning for Strategic Leadership.*
New Directions for Institutional Research, no. 52. San Francisco: Jossey-Bass, Winter 1986.

the University of North Carolina, Chapel Hill. In "Establishing an Environmental Scanning Process" (1985), he proposes that a college or university create a formal environmental scanning system "designed to identify emerging issues, events, or trends that portend threats to and opportunities for the institution." To do so, he recommends organizing a "scanning committee" that should systematically collect data from a variety of sources and then evaluate "the implications of these data for action by the chief executive officer" (p. 21). For other relevant writings by Morrison, see the references to his work and to that of Morrison and others (1983, 1984) at the end of this chapter.

Other writers on scanning in higher education include Collier (1980, 1981), Cope (1978, 1981), Glover and Holmes (1983), Hearn and Heydinger (1985). In addition, Glenny and Bowen (1980) discuss a variety of indicators that they believe deserve attention—both long-range, such as shifts in the socioeconomic and ethnic mix of the population, and short-term, such as changes in average student loads.

Sources of Data on the Demographic Environment

National Data. The Bureau of the Census of the Department of Commerce is obviously the nation's foremost primary source of population and economic data. For information on its new publications, computer tape files, microfiche, and maps, see its free *Monthly Product Announcement.* To be placed on the mailing list, write to the Data User Services Division, Customer Services (Publications), Bureau of the Census, Washington, D.C. 20233.

In its monthly *Data User News,* the bureau reports on selected recent publications and census developments. For an annual subscription at $21, write to the Superintendent of Documents, Government Printing Office, Washington, D.C. 20401; telephone (202) 783-3238.

The bureau also has a telephone contact list for its staff specialists, who can answer specific questions. For a copy of this list, call User Training, in the Data User Services Division, (301) 763-1510. The bureau's general customer service number is (301) 763-4100. Information on the bureau's on-line data service, CENDATA, can be obtained from the CENDATA Staff, Data User Services Division, Bureau of the Census, Washington, D.C. 20233. CENDATA is available to subscribers of DIALOG Information Services, 3460 Hillview Avenue, Palo Alto, California 94304—telephone (800) 227-1927; in California (800) 982-5838—or from The Glimpse Corporation, 125 South Royal Street, Alexandria, Virginia 22314; telephone (703) 836-6800.

Other Sources of National Data. The journal of the Demographic Institute, *American Demographics*—available from P.O. Box 68, Ithaca, New York 14815; telephone (607) 273-6343—contains many useful articles, such as Ehrenhalt (1983), Smith (1983), and Robey and Russel (1984). The institute also publishes a newsletter, *The Numbers News,* to keep its members informed about new demographic information, much of it from the Census Bureau.

In Washington, D.C., the Population Reference Bureau, Inc., publishes its *Population Bulletin,* with such relevant articles as those of Biggar (1979) and Davis and others (1983).

At the Institute for Educational Leadership, Inc., in Washington, D.C., Senior Fellow Harold L. Hodgkinson has been studying national demographic changes in the states as these changes relate to high school and college enrollment and retention rates. His report, *All One System: Demographics of Education—Kindergarten Through Graduate School,* has been published by the institute at Suite 310, 1001 Connecticut Avenue N.W., Washington, D.C. 20036; telephone (202) 822-8405.

Other useful sources of national social and economic data include the Rand Corporation (see, for example, Butz and others, 1982) and the National Center for Higher Education Management Systems (for example, Christal, 1983).

State-Level Data. Each state has its own official repository of population and economic statistics, as well as its own liaison with the federal Census Bureau. As examples, Washington State's official agency is its Office of Financial Management; Oregon's is the Oregon Census Bureau at Portland State University; and California's is the State Department of Finance, which in 1983 issued population forecasts by county through the year 2020. From such agencies, you can usually obtain school enrollment forecasts and annual age-specific cohort estimates by county—including, for example, the percentage of minority residents and of those aged sixty-five and older. For a list of the designated census data centers in all fifty states, write to Linda Gage, Population Research Unit, California State Department of Finance, 1025 P Street, Sacramento, California 95814.

Local Data. Useful data on local demographic trends can usually be obtained from city and county planning commissions and major banks. Metropolitan region organizations—such as, in California, the Southern California Association of Governments and the Association of Bay Area Governments—also have helpful data.

Sources of Data on the Economic Environment

National Data. Beyond publications of the Bureau of the Census, the major periodical resource on economic trends is *Economic Indicators,* published for the federal Council of Economic Advisers by the U.S. Government Printing Office. An annual projection of the national economy is produced by the Graduate School of Management of the University of California, Los Angeles, as the *UCLA Business Forecast.*

Regional Data. Regional economic data are available from the twelve regional offices of the Federal Reserve System, as well as from such diverse regional and interstate agencies as the Tennessee Valley Authority, in the Southeast, and the Bonneville Power Administration, in the Pacific Northwest.

State-Level Data. Each state operates an official economic and revenue forecast agency. For example, in Washington State, the Economic and Revenue Forecast Council produces quarterly economic forecasts through the Research and Information Division of the Department of Revenue. The major banks in each region produce annual economic analyses. In the Pacific Northwest, for instance, colleges and universities rely on the studies of the Rainier Bank and Seattle First National Bank, among others; in California, on those (among others) of the Bank of America and Security Pacific Bank. In some states, private research organizations, such as the Center for Continuing Study of the California Economy, in Palo Alto, specialize in economic analyses. In most if not all states, interpretations of economic and social trends are issued by departments or units of public universities. In Washington State, for example, Annabel Kirschner Cook, extension sociologist in the Department of Rural Sociology and census data coordinator of the Social Research Center of Washington State University, issues a periodical newsletter, *Census Notes,* on county-by-county trends.

Local Data. Useful data on local economic trends can usually be obtained from city and county tax boards and chambers of commerce, as well as from major local banks.

Sources of Data on the Political Environment

Frequent sources of information on national political trends affecting colleges and universities are *The Chronicle of Higher Education* and the American Council on Education's *Higher Education and National Affairs.* At the state level, appropriations for higher education are a major barometer of political trends affecting colleges and universities. For national summaries of these state appropriations, the Bureau of the Census is a primary source through its annual surveys of state government finances, as are the Center for Statistics of the Office of Education Research and Improvement; the U.S. Department of Education, through its Integrated Postsecondary Education Data System; Ed Hines, through *Grapevine* (available from the Department of Educational Administration and Foundations, Illinois State University, Normal, Illinois 61761); and John Minter Associates.

Making use of these data, the National Association of State Universities and Land-Grant Colleges publishes *Appropriations of State Tax Funds for Operating Expenses of Higher Education.* D. Kent Halstead of the Office of Educational Research and Improvement in the Department of Education writes his annual *State Profiles: Financing Public Higher Education,* the 1985–1986 volume of which is available for $12.50 from Research Associates of Washington, 2605 Klingle Road N.W., Washington, D.C. 20008. The Center for Statistics of the Department of Education publishes *Statistical Highlight: Expenditures of State and Local Governments,* based on its financial statistics of institutions of higher education survey. Peat, Marwick, Mitchell & Co. uses the John Minter Associates data for their *Ratio Analysis in Higher Education,* and *The Chronicle of Higher Education* produces its *Fact File: Appropriations for Higher Education.*

Among other sources of state financial data are the National Education Association, through its *Rankings of the States* (1984) and Marilyn McCoy and D. Kent Halstead, in the fourth edition of their *Higher Education Financing in the Fifty States* (1984).

Data on the Organizational Environment of Higher Education

National Data. The most comprehensive data on national trends among colleges and universities, as organizations or institutions, stem from the annual Integrated Postsecondary Education Data System surveys of the Center for Statistics. References to a variety of these data and other data sources appear in the newly published *Comparative Data about Higher Education: A Resource Directory* of the State Higher Education Executive Officers (SHEEO) Association, Suite 310, 1860 Lincoln Street, Denver, Colorado 80295; telephone (303) 830-3685. In addition, several other organizations are useful sources of data on two particularly important organizational areas, comparative faculty salaries and tuition and fees:

- National data on faculty salaries are gathered by Maryse Eymonerie Associates (P.O. Box 520, McLean, Virginia 22101), the College and University Personnel Association (Suite 120, 11 Dupont Circle, Washington, D.C. 20036), the Office of Institutional Research of Oklahoma State University (Stillwater, Oklahoma 74074)—for land-grant colleges and state universities only—and by the American Association of Community and Junior Colleges (Suite 410, One Dupont Circle, Washington, D.C. 20036) for two-year colleges. Results of these surveys are published by the respective agencies and also appear in *Academe,* published by the American Association of University Professors, and in *The Chronicle of Higher Education* "Fact File."
- National data on tuition and fees are gathered by the American Association of State Colleges and Universities, The College Board, Higher Education Publications, Inc., John Minter Associates, Inc., the Center for Statistics of the U.S. Department of Education, and the University of Wisconsin–Madison (the latter for state universities and land-grant colleges). They are published by the respective organizations or by the National

Association of State Universities and Land-Grant Colleges, *The Chronicle of Higher Education,* and other agencies.

Regional Data. Regional data on colleges and universities are available from the nation's three higher education regional interstate agencies.

In New England, see *Facts about New England Colleges, Universities, and Institutes* of the New England Board of Higher Education (40 Grove Street, Wellesley, Massachusetts 02181), published about every three years.

Among relevant publications of the Southern Regional Education Board (130 Sixth Street N.W., Atlanta, Georgia 30313) are its *SREB-State Data Exchange with State Higher Education Agencies, Fact Book on Higher Education in the South,* its several *Tuition and Fees* reports, and its *Tuition Policy for the Eighties* (1981).

For publications of WICHE, the Western Interstate Commission for Higher Education (P.O. Drawer P, Boulder, Colorado 80302), see Dolman and Kaufman (1984) and McConnell and Kaufman (1984), as well as WICHE's *A Profile of Higher Education in the West* (1981) and *Tuition and Fees in Public Higher Education in the West.*

State-Level Data. State higher education agencies periodically report enrollment trends and forecasts. As examples, see *Enrollment Forecasts 1985-95* of the Coordinating Board, Texas College and University System (1984), the *New Jersey Enrollment Projection Model* of the New Jersey State Department of Higher Education (n.d.), the "Enrollment Projection Analysis" of the State Council of Higher Education for Virginia (1983), and Presley (1983, 1984).

Institutional Data. For assessing the internal environment of institutions, most institutional researchers are familiar with many techniques, ranging from standardized survey instruments, such as the Institutional Functioning Inventory and the Institutional Goals Inventory of The Educational Testing Service, to the value audits of the Society for Values in Higher Education, but various approaches can be found in Jedamus and Peterson (1980).

Data on the Technological Environment

Of all current technological developments, the computer seems to be having the greatest impact on academic institutions. Computer buffs tend to rely on the weekly *Computer World* and the monthly *Datamation* as published sources of current news, and several report that for computer specialists, the most useful source of annual updated materials is Datapro Research Corporation, 1805 Underwood Boulevard, Delran, New Jersey 08075; telephone (609) 764-0100. For technological developments in general affecting higher education, *The Chronicle of Higher Education* occasionally includes wide-ranging interpretive articles.

Data on the Social-Cultural Environment

In his chapter, Jonsen lists several useful books, published earlier this decade, about current social-cultural trends with implications for colleges and universities. Data on such trends are available from most of the major sources already listed here for the demographic and economic environment. Interpretations of these data, as well as the insights of social observers and social critics on emerging trends, appear continually in the mass media and in the professional periodicals. Good information on these trends can often be obtained from conversations with colleagues in such academic disciplines as American studies, history, and the behavioral sciences.

Changes in student attitudes and values may be noted in the data collected through the annual freshman surveys of the Cooperative Institutional Research Program (CIRP). The data are available from Alexander W. Astin, Graduate School of Education, University of California, Los Angeles, California 90027; telephone (213) 825-1925.

Finally, longitudinal data on the high school–college transition and college and postcollege experiences of recent cohorts of students are available from C. Dennis Carroll, with the "High School and Beyond" study of the Educational Outcomes Division, Center for Statistics, Office of Education Research and Improvement, U.S. Department of Education; telephone (202) 254-7361. Carroll also has information on a new national educational longitudinal study, to be launched by the division in 1988 and to follow students into the 1990s. Also available from his office are National Assessment of Educational Progress annual data on changes in the knowledge, skills, understandings, and academic achievements of young people.

References

Aguilar, F. J. *Scanning the Business Environment.* New York: Macmillan, 1967.

Biggar, J. C. "The Sunning of America: Migration to the Sunbelt." *Population Bulletin,* 1979, *34* (1), (entire issue).

Butz, W. P., McCarthy, K. F., Morrison, P. A., and Vaiana, M. E. *Demographic Challenges in America's Future.* Santa Monica, Calif.: The Rand Corporation, 1982.

Camillus, J. C. "Corporate Strategy and Executive Action: Transition Stages and Linkage Dimensions." *Academy of Management Review,* 1981, *6* (2), 253–259.

Christal, M. E. *Enrollment Analysis at the State Level.* Boulder, Colo.: National Center for Higher Education Management Systems, 1983.

Collier, D. "Strategic Planning for Colleges and Universities: The Strategic Academic Unit Approach." Duplicated paper. Boulder, Colo.: National Center for Higher Education Management Systems, 1980.

Collier, D. "The Applicability of the Strategic Planning Concept to Colleges and Universities." Duplicated paper. Boulder, Colo.: National Center for Higher Education Management Systems, 1981.

Coordinating Board, Texas College and University System. *Enrollment Forecasts 1985-95: Texas Institutions of Higher Education.* Austin, Texas: Coordinating Board, 1984.

Cope, R. G. *Strategic Policy Planning: A Guide for College and University Administrators.* Littleton, Colo.: Ireland Education Corporation, 1978.

Cope, R. G. "Environmental Assessments for Strategic Planning." In N. L. Poulton (ed.), *Evaluation of Management and Planning Systems.* New Directions for Institutional Research, no. 31. San Francisco: Jossey-Bass, 1981.

Davis, G., Haub, C., and Willette, J. "U.S. Hispanics: Changing the Face of America." *Population Bulletin,* 1983, *38* (3), (entire issue).

Dolman, G., Jr., and Kaufman, N. S. *The Changing Demographics of the Southwest States.* Boulder, Colo.: WICHE Information Clearinghouse, 1984.

Drucker, P. *Managing in Turbulent Times.* New York: Harper & Row, 1980.

Ehrenhalt, S. M. "What Lies Ahead for College Graduates?" *American Demographics,* 1983, *5* (10), 29-33.

Glenny, L. A., and Bowen, F. M. *Signals for Change: Stress Indicators for Colleges and Universities.* Sacramento: California Postsecondary Education Commission, 1980.

Glover, R. H., and Holmes, J. "Assessing the External Environment." In N. P. Uhl (ed.), *Using Research for Strategic Planning.* New Directions for Institutional Research, no. 37. San Francisco: Jossey-Bass, 1983.

Hearn, J. C., and Heydinger, R. B. "Scanning the External Environment of a University: Objectives, Constraints, and Possibilities." *Journal of Higher Education,* 1985, *56* (4), 419-445.

Hegarty, W. H. "Strategic Planning in the 1980s: Coping with Complex External Forces." *Planning Review,* 1981, *9* (1), 9-12.

Heydinger, R. B. "Institutional Research and Planning: Is Futures Research the Next Step?" In J. L. Morrison, W. L. Renfro, and W. I. Boucher (eds.), *Applying Methods and Techniques of Futures Research.* New Directions for Institutional Research, no. 39. San Francisco: Jossey-Bass, 1983.

Hodgkinson, H. L. *All One System: Demographics of Education—Kindergarten Through Graduate School.* Washington, D.C.: Institute for Educational Leadership, 1985.

Jedamus, P., Peterson, M. W., and others. *Improving Academic Management.* San Francisco: Jossey-Bass, 1980.

Kast, F. "Scanning the Future Environment: Social Indicators." *California Management Review,* 1980, *23,* 22-32.

Lorange, P. "Strengthening Organizational Capacity to Execute Strategic Change." In J. M. Pennings and Associates (ed.), *Organizational Strategy and Change.* San Francisco: Jossey-Bass, 1985.

McConnell, W. R., and Kaufman, N. S. *High School Graduates: Projections for the Fifty States (1982-2000).* Boulder, Colo.: Western Interstate Commission for Higher Eduation, 1984.

McCoy, M., and Halstead, D. K. *Higher Education Financing in the Fifty States: Interstate Comparisons, Fiscal Year 1982.* (4th ed.) Boulder, Colo.: National Center for Higher Education Management Systems, National Institute of Education, 1984.

Morrison, J. L. "Establishing an Environmental Scanning Process." In R. M. Davis (ed.), *Leadership and Institutional Renewal.* New Directions for Higher Education, no. 49. San Francisco: Jossey-Bass, 1985.

Morrison, J. L., Renfro, W. L., and Boucher, W. I. (eds.). *Applying Methods and Techniques of Futures Research.* New Directions for Institutional Research, no. 39. San Francisco: Jossey-Bass, 1983.

Morrison, J. L., Renfro, W. L., and Boucher, W. I. *Futures Research and the Strategic Planning Process: Implications for Higher Education.* ASHE/ERIC Research Report Series, no. 7. Washington, D.C.: Association for the Study of Higher Education, 1984.

Nanus, B. "QUEST—Quick Environmental Scanning Techniques." *Long-Range Planning,* 1982, *15* (2), 39–45.

National Education Association, Professional and Organizational Development/Research Division. *Data Search: Rankings of the States, 1984.* Washington, D.C.: National Education Association, 1984.

New Jersey State Department of Higher Education. *New Jersey Enrollment Projection Model.* Trenton: New Jersey State Department of Higher Education, no date.

Presley, J. B. *An Analysis of Enrollment Trends in Connecticut Higher Education: 1982.* Report of the Board of Governors, Department of Education, State of Connecticut. Hartford: The Board of Governors, 1983.

Presley, J. B. *Demographic Changes and Their Impact on Enrollment in Connecticut Higher Education: 1983–2000.* Report of the Board of Governors, Department of Education, State of Connecticut. Hartford: The Board of Governors, 1984.

Renfro, W. L. "Detecting Signals of Change: The Environmental Scanning Process." *The Futurist,* 1984, *18* (4), 49–56.

Robey, B., and Russel, C. "Trends: All Americans." *American Demographics,* 1984, *6* (2), 89–98.

Smith, H. L. "Higher Education's Future." *American Demographics,* 1983, *5* (10), 22–48.

Southern Regional Education Board. *Tuition Policy for the Eighties.* Atlanta: Southern Regional Education Board, 1981.

Southern Regional Education Board. *Fact Book on Higher Education in the South, 1983 and 1984.* Atlanta: Southern Regional Education Board, 1984.

Southern Regional Education Board. *SREB—State Data Exchange with State Higher Education Agencies, 1983–84.* Atlanta: Southern Regional Education Board, 1984.

State Council of Higher Education for Virginia. "Enrollment Projection Analysis, Commonwealth of Virginia. Case Study, October 1983." Duplicated Report. Richmond: State Council of Higher Education, 1983.

Vanderwicken, R. "'Externalysis': A New Dimension in Planning." *Planning Review,* July 1982, *45,* 24–27.

Western Interstate Commission for Higher Education. *A Profile of Higher Education in the West.* Boulder, Colo.: Western Interstate Commission for Higher Education, 1981.

Western Interstate Commission for Higher Education. *Tuition and Fees in Public Higher Education in the West.* Boulder, Colo.: Western Interstate Commission for Higher Education, no date.

Martin M. Ahumada is a postsecondary education specialist at the California Postsecondary Education Commission. Previously, he served as higher education policy analyst at the Education Commission of the States in Denver, Colorado.

JB Lon Hefferlin has served as editor of publications for the California Postsecondary Education Commission since 1981. Before 1981, he was higher education editor for Jossey-Bass Inc.

Index

R

S

T

U

V

W

Y

U.S. Postal Service

STATEMENT OF OWNERSHIP, MANAGEMENT AND CIRCULATION

1. Title of Publication: New Directions for Institutional Research	Publication No.: 0 9 8 8 3 0	2. Date of Filing: 9/26/86
3. Frequency of Issue: Quarterly	No. of Issues Published Annually: 4	Annual Subscription Price: $30 indv/$40 inst

4. Complete Mailing Address of Known Office of Publication: 433 California St., San Francisco (SF County), CA 94104

5. Complete Mailing Address of the Headquarters of General Business Offices of the Publisher: 433 California St., San Francisco (SF County), CA 94104

6. Full Names and Complete Mailing Address of Publisher, Editor, and Managing Editor

Publisher: Jossey-Bass Inc., Publishers, 433 California St., S.F., CA 94104

Editor: Patrick T. Terenzini, Institute of Higher Education, University of Georgia, Athens, Georgia 30602

Managing Editor: Allen Jossey-Bass, 433 California St., San Francisco, CA 94104

7. Owner [illegible]

Full Name	Complete Mailing Address
Jossey-Bass Inc., Publishers	433 California St., S.F., CA 94104

For names and addresses of stockholders, see attached list.

8. [illegible]

Full Name	Complete Mailing Address

9. [illegible]

10. Extent and Nature of Circulation

Extent and Nature of Circulation	Average No. Copies Each Issue During Preceding 12 Months	Actual No. Copies of Single Issue Published Nearest to Filing Date
A. Total No. Copies	1900	1930
B. [illegible] 1. [illegible]	391	2
2. [illegible]	888	712
C. [illegible]	1279	714
D. [illegible]	87	185
E. [illegible]	1366	899
F. [illegible] 1. [illegible]	534	1031
2. [illegible]		
G. Total [illegible]	1900	1930

11. I certify that the statements made by me above are correct and complete — [signature] Vice President

PS Form 3526